George Segal
Street Scenes

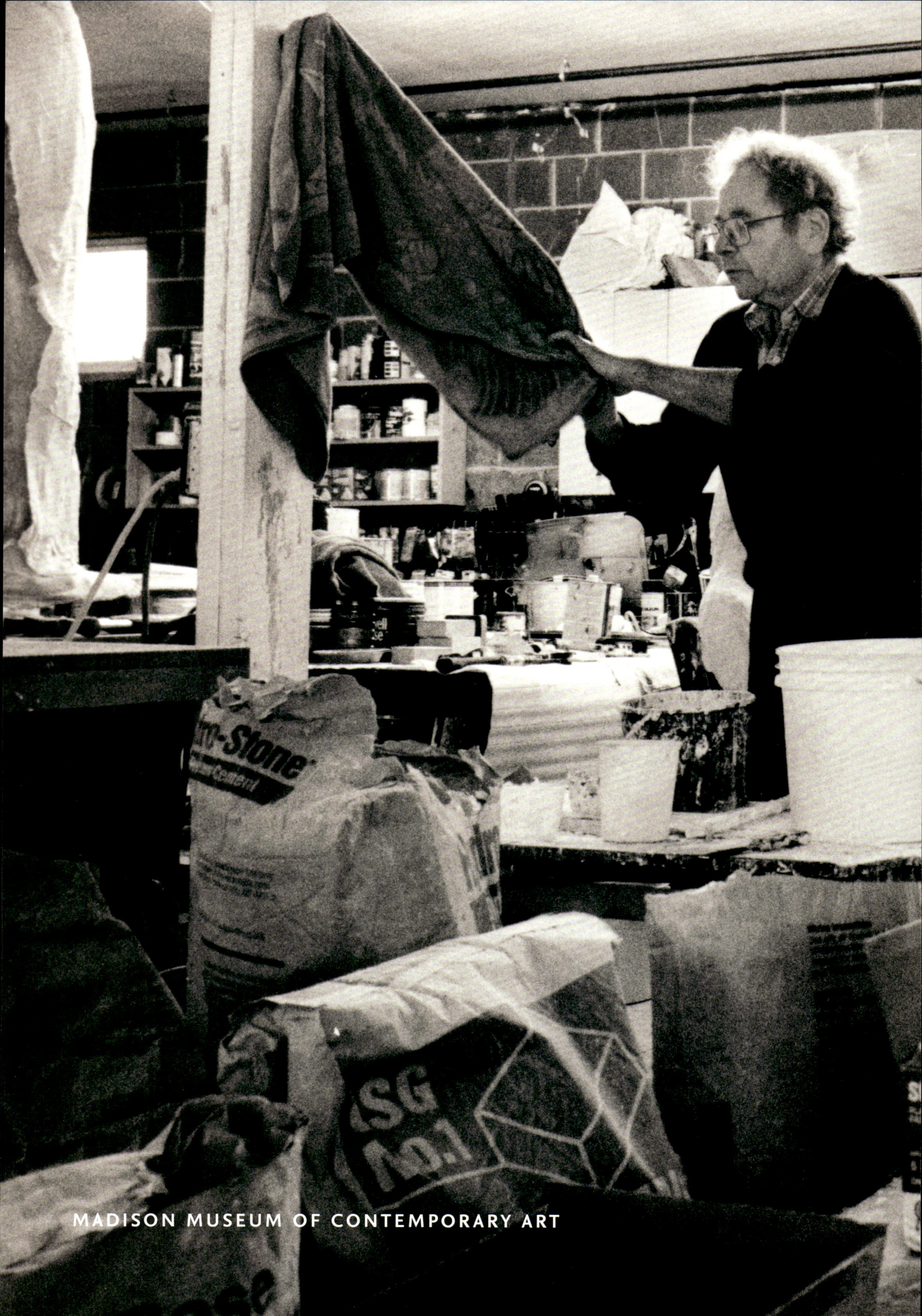
MADISON MUSEUM OF CONTEMPORARY ART

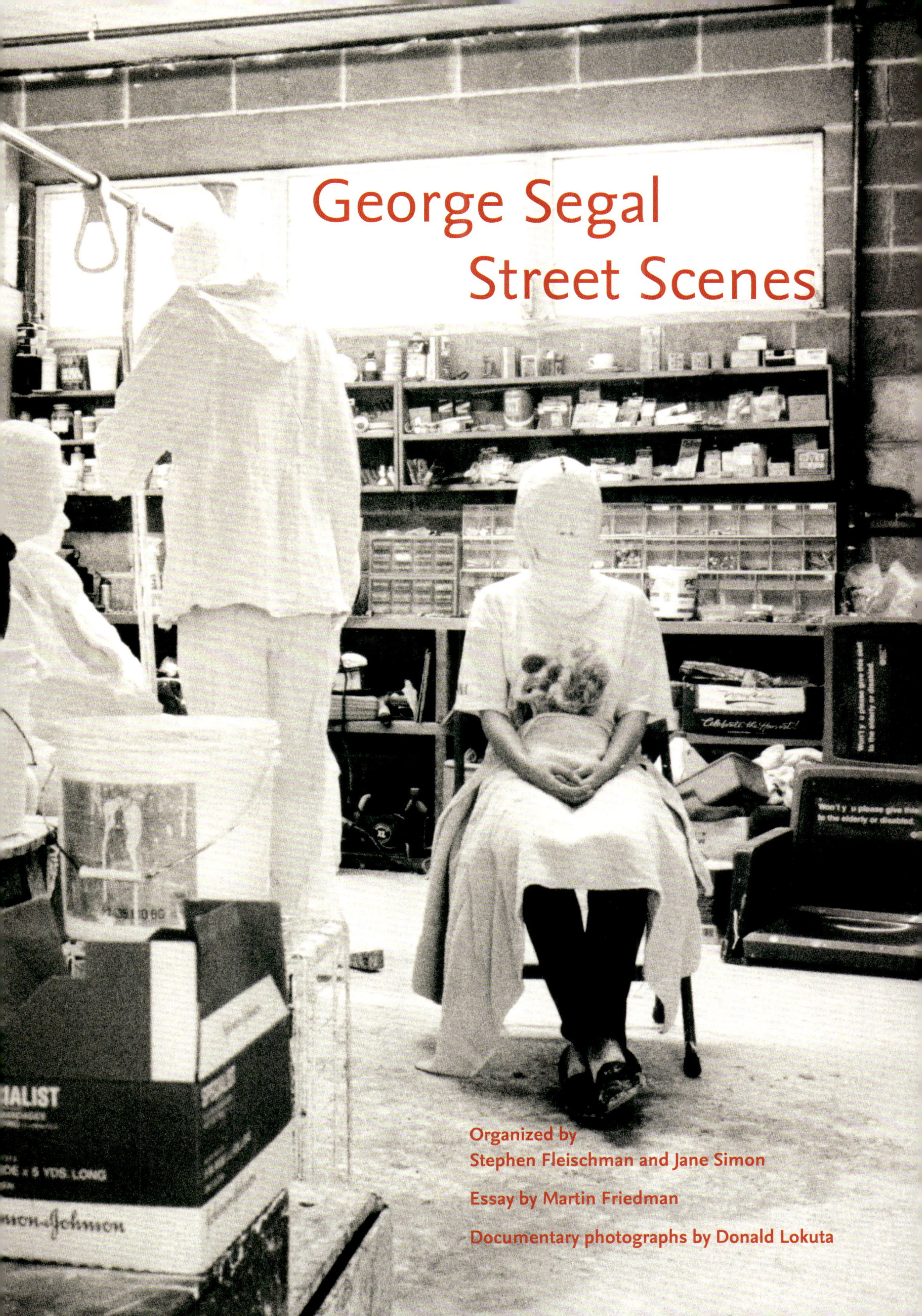

George Segal
Street Scenes

Organized by
Stephen Fleischman and Jane Simon

Essay by Martin Friedman

Documentary photographs by Donald Lokuta

Published for the exhibition *George Segal: Street Scenes.*
Organized by the Madison Museum of Contemporary Art, Madison, Wisconsin.

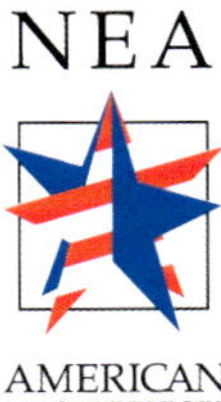

Generous funding for *George Segal: Street Scenes* has been provided by the
National Endowment for the Arts; Bill and Jan DeAtley; Whyte Hirschboeck Dudek S.C.;
Daniel Erdman; Associated Bank; the Steinhauer Charitable Trust; J.H. Findorff & Son;
CUNA Mutual Group; the Dane County Cultural Affairs Commission with additional funds
from the Overture Foundation; Gina and Michael Carter; a grant from the
Wisconsin Arts Board, with funds from the State of Wisconsin and the National Endowment
for the Arts; and the Art League of the Madison Museum of Contemporary Art.

Madison Museum of Contemporary Art
Madison, Wisconsin
September 13 – December 28, 2008

Nasher Sculpture Center
Dallas, Texas
January 24 – April 5, 2009

The Nelson-Atkins Museum of Art
Kansas City, Missouri
May 9 – August 2, 2009

Norton Museum of Art
West Palm Beach, Florida
September 8–December 6, 2009

Library of Congress
Cataloging-in-Publication Data

George Segal, 1924–2000
  George Segal : street scenes.
  p. cm.
  ISBN 978-0-913883-34-1
  1. Segal, George, 1924–2000 –
  Exhibitions.
  2. Streets in art – Exhibitions.
  3. City and town life in art –
  Exhibitions.
  I. Madison Museum of
  Contemporary Art (Madison, Wis.)
  II. Title.
  NB237.S44A4 2008
  730.92 – dc22
  2008008595

Copyright © 2008
Madison Museum of Contemporary Art
227 State Street, Madison, Wisconsin
53703

Distributed worldwide by
D.A.P./Distributed Art Publishers, Inc.
155 Sixth Avenue, 2nd floor
New York, New York 10013
Telephone: 212 627 1999
Fax: 212 627 9484
dap@dapinc.com
www.artbook.com

Edition 3,500

Copyeditor
Paula Cooper, Madison, Wisconsin

Designer
Lorraine Ferguson, New York, New York

Printer
Oceanic Graphic Press, China

A Braille version of this catalogue is
available upon request. Please contact
the Madison Museum of Contemporary
Art Education Department.

Cover
George Segal (American, 1924–2000)
Depression Bread Line 1991
Bronze
Installed at Grounds For Sculpture,
Hamilton, New Jersey

Title spread
George Segal working on
Bus Passengers 1997
Photograph by Donald Lokuta.

Contents

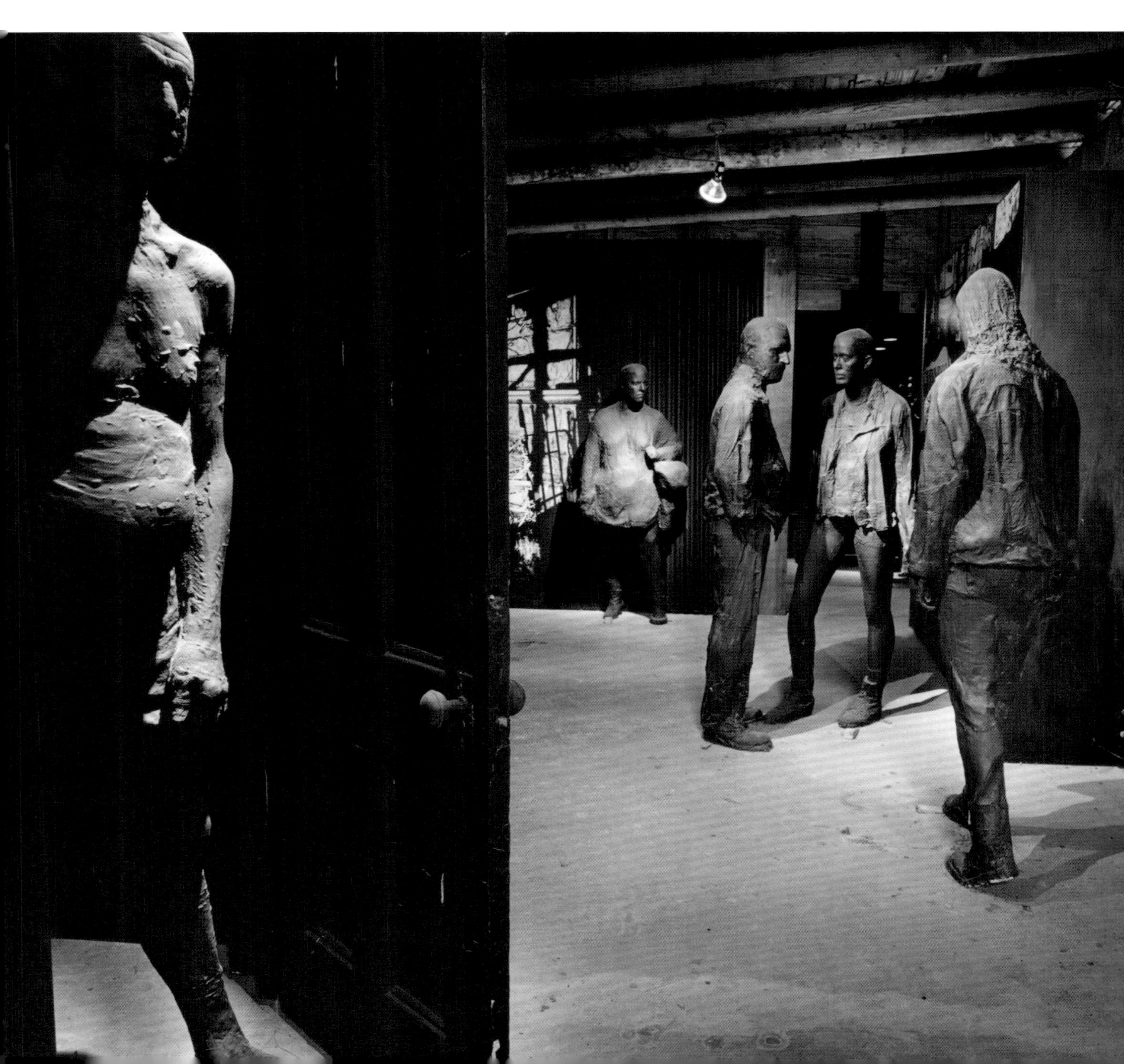

View of room #7 in
George Segal's studio, 2000

Stephen Fleischman

Director's Foreword

Driving through the Holland Tunnel into industrial
sections of New Jersey provided few clues about
my destination. I was going to a former chicken farm,
where the sculptor George Segal had lived and
worked for some sixty years, before his death in 2000.
It was Thursday, September 28, 2006, and I was to meet
with the members of The George and Helen Segal
Foundation: Helen, George's wife of fifty-four years,
their daughter, Rena, and niece, Susan Kutliroff.
I was fortunate to have received an introduction from
my former employer and friend, Martin Friedman,
who had been one of George's closest confidants.

As I headed toward New Brunswick, the
traffic eased and the landmarks became slightly more
suburban. It was still a gritty landscape filled with
ordinary places and people. It occurred to me that I
was driving through the terrain of George Segal,
a drive or bus ride he made thousands of times from
New Jersey to New York City and back again. Segal
was an artist who almost always worked from his
immediate surroundings, so in effect I was experi-
encing the underpinnings of his work.

I made the drive with great anticipation. My
enthusiasm for George Segal's sculpture had been
piqued in 1983, when I moved to Minneapolis to work
at the Walker Art Center. His pivotal work *The Diner*,
1964–66, was on long-term view in Gallery 5 with
other key objects from the permanent collection. The
sculpture is embedded in my mind: a lone stool
beneath a stark fluorescent light inhabited by a rough-
hewn man in plaster eating pie and drinking coffee,
while the waitress fills another cup. Later, the Walker
Art Center acquired *Walking Man*, 1988, to install in the

Minneapolis Sculpture Garden across the street from the museum. Segal was one of the most collected sculptors of his generation, and I have been fortunate to encounter his work frequently on my travels.

The Segal farm is not noteworthy from its exterior. It is located on a once-rural road that has become increasingly congested with time. The home is warm and welcoming, but it gives no real hint of what awaits in the main outbuilding, where the chickens once roosted. This long, unassuming building is installed much as it was when Segal was alive. To enter it is to be overwhelmed with a feeling of history. The ten rooms of the building feature a wide selection of Segal's drawings, plaster fragments, relief sculptures, and major sculptural installations. Going from the outside to the inside of the structure is to experience the opening of George Segal's universe (p. 6). Everywhere figures sit, stand, and lie, interacting with their carefully fabricated environments and by extension the neighboring installations. The many sculptures are evidence of the artist's interest in ordinary people engaged in everyday routines. Much of it captured on his frequent trips to New York City, Segal used the people, places, and objects that surrounded him to make sculpture that touches a universal chord.

The rooms of the building continue at length, slowly unveiling an astonishingly rich body of work. The drawings and sculptures are testimony to Segal's prolific career. The artist was, according to all accounts and as explained in the essay by Martin Friedman that follows, an incorrigible scavenger. His works are filled with furniture, appliances, street signs, and scraps of wood and metal. Within that former chicken coop, the interests and aesthetic sensibilities of George Segal still reside.

Jane Simon, curator of exhibitions for MMoCA, and I have served as co-curators of this show. Our frequent discussions helped shape the concept of the exhibition. During his distinguished career, George Segal had many solo exhibitions around the world. A number of these were traveling surveys of his work. It became increasingly clear that the exhibition at the Madison Museum of Contemporary Art would benefit from the examination of a specific aspect of the artist's work. *George Segal: Street Scenes* explores the artist's long and passionate relationship with the urban environment and his profound interest in typical scenes on the street and the interaction of ordinary human beings. The theme "street scenes" cuts across his many decades of artistic activity and allows audiences an opportunity to fully engage with his work.

I am grateful to Helen, Rena, and Susan for their full cooperation and encouragement throughout the project. The George and Helen Segal Foundation and Carroll Janis, New York agreed to provide the core loans for this major traveling exhibition. In addition to the Foundation, it is a pleasure to thank the other lenders to this exhibition, who parted with important works for an extended period of time: the Albright-Knox Art Gallery, Buffalo, New York; the Museum of Contemporary Art, Chicago; The Newark Museum, Newark, New Jersey; the Walker Art Center, Minneapolis; and the Whitney Museum of American Art, New York.

I am also grateful to The George and Helen Segal Foundation for gifting to MMoCA a cast of *Depression Bread Line,* one of the artist's seminal works. This sculpture depicts five shabbily dressed men waiting for food in front of a wall and doorway. The original cast is a permanent part of the Franklin Delano Roosevelt Memorial in Washington, D.C. After the exhibition tour, this work will become part of the permanent collection of MMoCA. In addition to the Segal Foundation, it is a pleasure to acknowledge the generous contributions of Bill and Jan DeAtley, James and Sylvia Vaccaro, the Madison Community Foundation, Jim and Cathie Burgess, the Pleasant T. Rowland Foundation, the Overture Foundation, and Tom and Martha Carter, who helped make the casting of this sculpture possible.

A number of individuals have made *George Segal: Street Scenes* a reality. Martin Friedman and Jane Simon have both contributed thoughtful essays to this volume, which has been elegantly designed by Lorraine Ferguson and carefully edited by Paula Cooper. Photographs documenting George Segal's influences were provided by his longtime friend, Donald Lokuta. Carroll Janis, the Segal Foundation's representative, and Jeanie Deans were a source of constant help and encouragement throughout the project.

It has been gratifying to collaborate with the venues participating in the tour of *George Segal: Street Scenes.* Special thanks are due to Jed Morse, acting chief curator at the Nasher Sculpture Center, Dallas; Marc F. Wilson, director and CEO at The Nelson-Atkins Museum, Kansas City; and Christina Orr-Cahall, executive director at the Norton Museum of Art, West Palm Beach.

The Madison presentation and national tour of *George Segal: Street Scenes* and this publication were made possible by generous contributions from the National Endowment for the Arts; Bill and Jan DeAtley; Whyte Hirschboeck Dudek S.C.; Daniel Erdman; Associated Bank; the Steinhauer Charitable Trust; J.H. Findorff & Son; CUNA Mutual Group; the Dane County Cultural Affairs Commission with additional funds from the Overture Foundation; Gina and Michael Carter; a grant from the Wisconsin Arts Board, with funds from the State of Wisconsin and the National Endowment for the Arts; and the Art League of the Madison Museum of Contemporary Art.

My thanks also go to the board of trustees of the Madison Museum of Contemporary Art for their continuing support, as well as independent registrar Rachel May, whose diligence and dedication was critical to the success of this project. Douglas Caulk provided great expertise in packing and crating many of the works for travel. Finally, I would like to thank the staff of the Madison Museum of Contemporary Art, especially Nicole Allen, director of development; Sheri Castelnuovo, curator of education; Carl Fuldner, curatorial assistant; Jennifer Holmes, assistant to the director; Katie Kazan, director of public information; Marilyn Sohi, registrar; and Mark Verstegen, technical services supervisor.

George Segal: Street Scenes continues MMoCA's tradition of organizing significant exhibitions for travel. This project expands on the study of one of America's most important sculptors of the twentieth century.

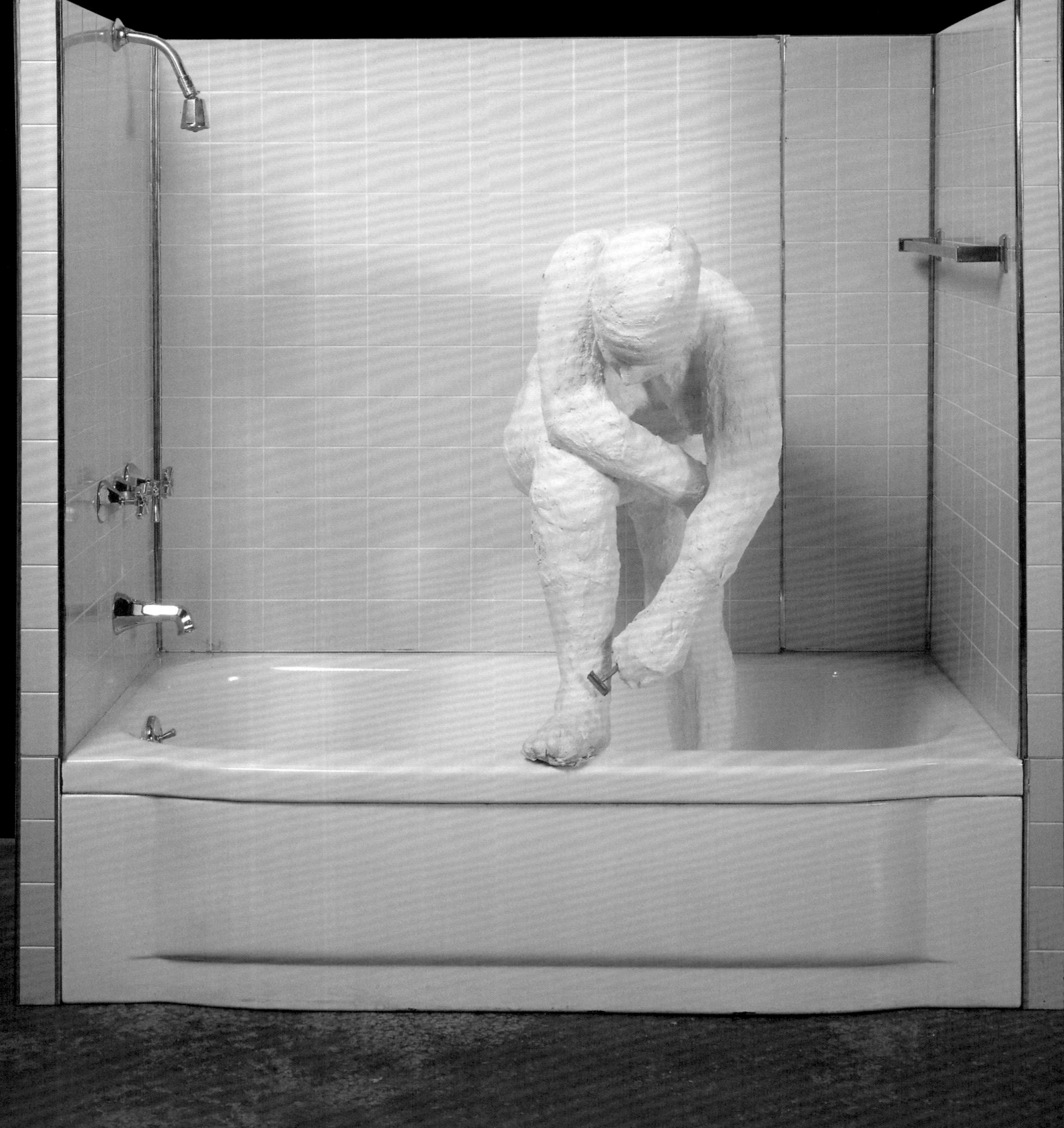

Martin Friedman

George's Blue-Collar Realism

Woman Standing in a Bathtub
1963
Muslin, plaster, wire mesh,
bathtub, metal fixtures,
linoleum tile, wood, razor
63 ¾ x 66 x 43 ½ inches
Private collection, San Francisco

A few months after the Walker Art Center's new building opened to the public, on May 18, 1971, there was a crisis in the galleries. One of our guards, Margaret, a fiftyish, matronly lady known for her welcoming smile, breathlessly made her way down the stairs to the lobby, where Stan Stepan, the museum's chief guard, was standing at his post. Margaret's face was deeply flushed. Something unspeakable had just happened in a gallery she had walked into while making her rounds. "It was terrible, just terrible!" she exclaimed, seeking to collect herself. "What happened, Margaret?" asked a concerned Stan, taking her hand and trying to calm her. Gradually regaining her composure, she said that upon entering a gallery she thought devoid of visitors, she could hear great thumping noises and groans coming from the far end. "They were coming from one of the sculptures," she said, narrowing her eyes, with a shudder. "You know, the one with those plaster people in the diner!" As she apprehensively approached the sculpture to investigate the cause of the noise, Margaret continued, what shocking sight did she see but two pairs of thrashing legs sticking out from behind the counter. "And when I looked down, I saw a man and a woman rolling around on the floor!" And what's more, she declared indignantly, "They were doing it!" When the now barely straight-faced Stan asked how she had handled this unusual situation, the outraged Margaret was more than ready for his question. She replied that she had addressed the offending couple in no uncertain terms, "Please, you two! Not on the art!"

George Segal loved this story and wanted to hear it over and over. It only proved, he said delightedly, just how much people connected with his work. Though the ardent couple's response may have been extreme, he was certainly right that the public identified with his art. For one thing, its subject matter was simultaneously immediate and universal. Its strength lay in its ordinariness. For another, his plaster figures were everyday people, not idealized; viewers could easily relate to them. It's understandable, as they were posed for by Segal's friends and family members.

George Segal's sculpture came to public attention during pop art's lively advent, in the late 1950s, but he was never emotionally at home in that rambunctious movement. His perception of the world differed markedly from that of his pop brethren, whose interests lay less in human interaction than in the magic of everyday objects. To that end, they freely appropriated images from supermarket shelves, the movies and television, the comics, and the fictional worlds of advertising. Though ordinary objects also made their way into Segal's sculptures, the human form was his enduring focus.

George was a genial, rumpled-looking man with a broad, friendly face and a mass of wiry black hair that remained thick, even as it grayed. He had a ready smile and a deep, easy laugh. Comfortable with everyone and anyone, he conversed animatedly with those he had just met as though they were old friends, and they responded with equal warmth. His casual wardrobe of short-sleeved shirts, well-worn tweed jackets (some with cigarette burns), paint-spattered chinos, and loosely tied tennis shoes served for all occasions, whether he was visiting friends, attending exhibition openings—including his own—or

working in his studio. For all his down-to-earth personality, though, George had a clear sense of himself as an artist with an important place in contemporary art.

Well before achieving fame for his plaster effigies, he was a painter who, from the mid- to late 1950s, exhibited at the Hansa Gallery, on Tenth Street, in Lower Manhattan. Though the Hansas's artists— among them the figurative painter Jan Müller, the "Happenings" impresario, Allan Kaprow, the pioneering junk sculptors Richard Stankiewicz and his companion, Jean Follett—worked in widely differing modes and materials, the spirit of abstract expressionism loomed large there. It was the common denominator. It was "the look, the touch, the belief in handmade forms," exemplified by that intuitive way of making art, George told me, that so enthralled them and shaped his own artistic direction.

Though regarded as a quintessential New York artist, Segal had not lived in the city since his youth. In 1940, his parents, Jacob and Sophie Segal, and his older brother, Morris, moved from the South Bronx to South Brunswick, New Jersey. The Segals were among a number of Socialist-minded, Jewish, working-class families aspiring to a healthful new life well away from the tumult and hardships of the city. They envisaged a communal, kibbutz-like way of life. George, then sixteen, did not accompany them but stayed with an aunt in Brooklyn so that he could finish high school. On their newly acquired land, his parents went into chicken farming, a risky venture at best, and especially so for recent urban émigrés from the other side of the Hudson. Insulated from the difficulties

his parents faced in adjusting to country living, George,
after completing high school, took art classes at
Cooper Union and Pratt Institute. When Morris was
drafted into the army, George left New York for
South Brunswick to help out on the farm. Arduous as
life among the chickens was, he managed to continue
his studies in the city and also took art classes at
Rutgers University in New Brunswick. He and Helen,
whom he had married in 1946, acquired their own
chicken farm, across the road from that of his parents.
It was a near-catastrophic decision. So demanding
and unprofitable was this venture that they soon
regretted what they had done. They came to loathe
everything about those birds, George told me with a
rueful chuckle. Seeking another way of making
a living, he decided on teaching. He enrolled in New
York University, where he earned a bachelor's degree
in art education in 1949. In the late 1950s, to support
his young family—he and Helen had two children,
Jeffrey and Rena, by then—he taught art and English at
local high schools. In 1958, the Segals were liberated
from their poultry-dominated servitude when they
sold off all their chickens. When the last bird was gone,
so great was their joy, he recalled, that they waltzed
ecstatically around the empty chicken house.

There was at least one felicitous outcome of
that ill-starred venture: the long, barracks-like building
that had housed the unlamented fowls proved an
ideal space for a studio. That part nearest the Segals's
house was quickly converted into one. In successive
years, George would fill the building's vast remaining
space—and that of a second leftover chicken-era
structure next to it—with sculptures, many of them

still installed as they were at the time of his death,
on June 14, 2000.

Preoccupied as Segal was with formal issues
such as volume and voids, surface and color, he was at
heart a storyteller, a creator of parables in which
ordinary events took on extraordinary connotations.
Though most of his subjects were reflections of
his surroundings, there were occasional forays into
classic studio themes—nudes and still lifes in
particular. Many of his sculptures have a mythical
dimension. A slender female nude standing beneath a
huge rock overhang is reminiscent of a nymph from
antiquity. Figures huddled at street crossings
could be souls in limbo. On occasion he turned to
biblical themes to make not-so-veiled observations
about contemporary life. One was Abraham about to
sacrifice his son Isaac at the command of the Lord.
The two sculptures he based on this subject, he
said, were about an older generation's readiness to
sacrifice its children in the cause of war. Most Segal
imagery, however, is less specific and less moralistic.
Its great strength, in my view, is its ambiguity,
because for all of its descriptiveness, it invites widely
different interpretations.

The human body was the armature on which
Segal shaped his sculptures, but what came forth from
his studio were never merely line-by-line renditions.
Too much was going on in his head, too many feelings
about the subjects he was dealing with, and—just as
important—too many concerns about traditional
formal issues to permit such rote translations. The fact
is, nothing is routine about his representations of
the body. Slight and not-so-slight distortions abound

throughout his sculptures—exaggerated contours, agitated surfaces, and sharply defined areas next to blurry ones. Metaphorically and stylistically his fingerprints are everywhere.

Given George's strong feelings about expressionist painting, why, then, did he wander so far from it and turn to sculpture, I asked as we were selecting works for inclusion in the Walker's 1978 exhibition. Because he felt trapped in an emotional and stylistic dilemma, he replied. He increasingly felt that his paintings were unresolved and lacked the coalescence of form he ardently sought. Dissatisfied with what he was accomplishing in two dimensions, he added another one. The transition from painting to sculpture was rough. In 1958, he arrived at a hybrid approach, where they had equal roles. Heaping masses of wet plaster on wood and chicken-wire frameworks, he fashioned three primal figures. He then positioned each plaster golem—his surrogates, he said—in front of its own huge canvas, whose surface he had covered with sweeping, bright-hued, abstract shapes. There he was—in triplicate—pondering his artistic future. These crudely assembled effigies represented what might be termed his brief neolithic, proto-plaster-figure period. These rudimentary beings soon gave way to far more descriptive renditions of the human form. Thus began his outside-casting technique, in which the model was wrapped, some nude, some clothed, in water-activated, plaster-permeated bandages, to which he added more wet plaster. Describing the method, Segal told me, "I worked the plaster with my fingers, controlling its running and dripping. I produced a literal-looking figure, with practically an abstract expressionist surface." It was these larger-than-life, bulky personages that first earned him critical acclaim, in the early 1960s. Seeking to make figures of greater verisimilitude, in the mid-1970s he developed an inside-casting process. The plaster shells he peeled from the body served as molds, which he filled with liquid plaster that hardened into close approximations of the models on which they were made. Impressive as those later pieces are in their detail, I feel they have less gravitas than the primal, outside-cast figures that preceded them. Consider, for instance, the *Man Sitting at a Table*, a 1961 self-portrayal. This ponderous figure is a forceful, archaic-looking presence. There is similar affecting awkwardness about *Woman Standing in a Bathtub*, a 1963 proletarian riff on the classic nude-emerging-from-the-bath (p. 10). Among the many other sculptures in this technique are figures sitting in seedy luncheonettes, waiting forever in phone booths, and sunning themselves on rooftops.

George's semirural New Jersey surroundings offered a ready supply of subjects. His take on the local scene, while undeniably empathetic, might be described as low-rent Norman Rockwell. However, the events and settings in his pieces are not limited by geography. What takes place in them could happen anywhere in America. In some, old people sit impassively on front porches of clapboard houses; in others, equally disengaged younger ones sit in bleak interiors. A man stands, as though distracted, at a pinball machine. A woman's face visible through the window of a bar is eerily illuminated, from one side by the flickering light of an old TV, from the other by the neon glow of a Budweiser sign.

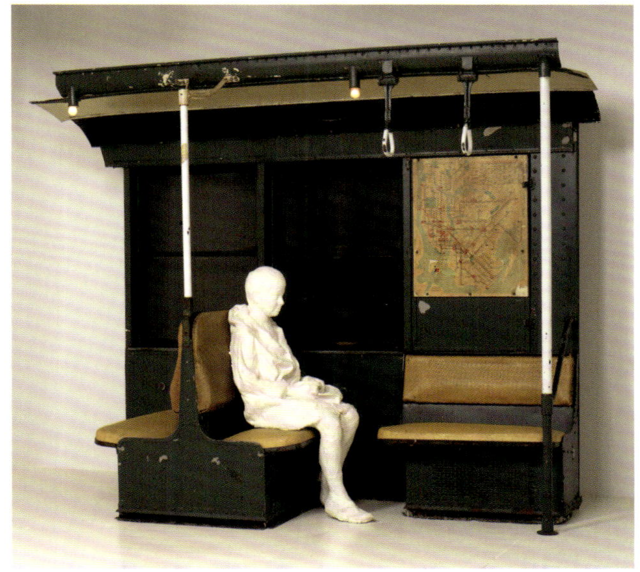

George gave a great deal of thought to selecting the architectural fragments and props for his pieces. An inveterate forager, he was always on the prowl for materials. Because he preferred those that bore traces of use, he was a frequenter of wrecking sites and secondhand stores. He not only hauled discarded furniture, salvaged doors, windows, and parts of staircases to his studio, but he also brought back larger, far more unwieldy treasures that caught his eye. Among them were entire cabins of abandoned trucks and buses, which were points of departure for sculptures.

For all Segal's absorption with small-town life, it was the city, with its restless energy and anonymity, that called to him—not only the New York he constantly commuted to but also the remembered cityscape from his youth. The precedents for his meditations on the city were not in sculpture, but in painting. His urban vignettes are a latter-day equivalent of the gritty American reportage found in the early twentieth-century canvases of John Sloan, Robert Henri, and their fellow Ashcan school literalists. In the 1930s and 40s, that descriptive mode, tempered by a sense of anomie, was to be found in Edward Hopper's city paintings. This was especially true of Hopper's bleak interiors with solitary figures, to which Segal's sparsely populated silent dramas are often likened.

Few of George's sculptures more pungently evoke his youth in the city than *The Butcher Shop,* a 1965 memoir of his apron-clad mother, cleaver in hand, hovering over a chicken on a chopping block. Equally arresting—if less dramatic—is *The Subway,* a 1968 essay in urban archaeology (p. 15). Seated in the subway car,

with its battered rattan seats, well-worn leather straps for standees, bare-bulb ceiling lights, and a vintage map on the wall is a phantomlike young woman on her way to nowhere. In Segal's more generalized city pieces, solitary men walk alongside boarded-up building sites, and others gaze, transfixed, into shop windows. The six pedestrians in *Rush Hour,* a 1983 plaster subsequently cast in bronze, wait for a nonexistent traffic signal to change (p. 17). Those who posed for its figures knew little about what the piece would be, George said. "All I told them was that it was wintertime and that they would be walking on a street with other people, but not any they knew. " Despite the psychological distance between them, they were close to each other compositionally, he said. Each figure was essential to the others, he pointed out, and in the final analysis the sculpture was about pure form.

A year before his retrospective at the Walker, George mused about his frequent drives to and from Manhattan. After a long day in the city, he said, he often stopped for coffee at a diner along the road, "so I could stay awake to finish the last leg of the journey. " *The Diner,* where Margaret famously found the offending couple, was an evocation of those late-night stops (pp. 26–27). A moody reflection on anonymous highway culture, its two chalk-white figures are on opposite sides of a long black counter. One is a burly man of uncertain age seated on a stool, the other, a waitress about to fill another cup from a coffee urn. They share the small space but seem unaware of each other, so absorbed are they in their own thoughts. Overhead, a fluorescent light bleakly illuminates the scene. The diner's vintage furnishings, George said, came from a restaurant that had just gone out of business. He talked about what might be taking place there, in film noir terms. "Two people alone after midnight—there's that electric danger. The waitress behind the counter is always sizing you up, wondering if you're going to rob her or rape her. So, there would be this careful avoidance of eye contact. "

He developed the ideas for such pieces in his head, as it were—never through preliminary drawings. Though he was an accomplished draughtsman, whose works on paper varied from large-scale, profusely detailed pencil and charcoal portraits of family members to thick-lined figure studies in colored chalk, his drawings had little to do with his sculptures. Rather, he composed those sculptures intuitively, with a sense of how they would look. When making a piece that involved more than one personage, he would experiment with configurations. For a long time he hauled heavy completed plasters around the studio, a task that grew more difficult over the years. Fortunately, Donald Lokuta, a photographer friend who had assisted George on a voluntary basis since 1984, was on hand for the heavy lifting.

Even as he worked on a sculpture, Segal thought about lighting. While many of his pieces are effective under general illumination, others were to be seen under highly controlled conditions. He often used light theatrically. A shaded bulb, like one over a pool table, makes barely visible the contours of the dark gray nude *Woman Sitting on a Bed*, 1993. When the 1992 *Street Crossing* (pp. 44–45) was shown at the Janis Gallery the year after it was made, George had the gallery walls painted black and its floor covered with

black tar paper. Visitors wandered among the brightly lit plaster pedestrians, moving in and out of their pools of light. Crucial as light can be in a Segal sculpture, color has a comparable, if not even more significant, role. It was inherent in the background architectural elements of the first outside-cast figures he made. Though these rough-surfaced beings dominated his production in the 1960s, the prospect of painting them from head to toe in bright color eventually proved irresistible. Certainly one of the most complex and confounding examples of such use of color was the *The Costume Party*, 1965, a strange collection of fantastically attired beings, each with a borrowed identity. Among them are an electric blue ass-headed personage, a woman in a black bodysuit sporting a white motorcycle helmet, a red-painted man wearing a framed photograph of himself around his neck, and a yellow-painted woman on a yellow chair. Conceivably, *The Costume Party*'s exotic array of figures baffled even George, to the point where he wasn't sure what to do with them. Not only did he keep changing the positions of his figures over six or seven years, but he also kept changing their color. I questioned whether he ever resolved the problem, even as he went on to paint other figures in brilliant hues. Thanks to color, in otherwise conventional studio compositions such as *The Corridor*, 1976, a luminous blue female nude standing between a red chair and a yellow door takes on surreal connotations. Color in this instance was another way of exploring what lay beyond reality.

No matter how fascinated George was with light and color, his art dealt primarily with the human condition. It all began with the selection of

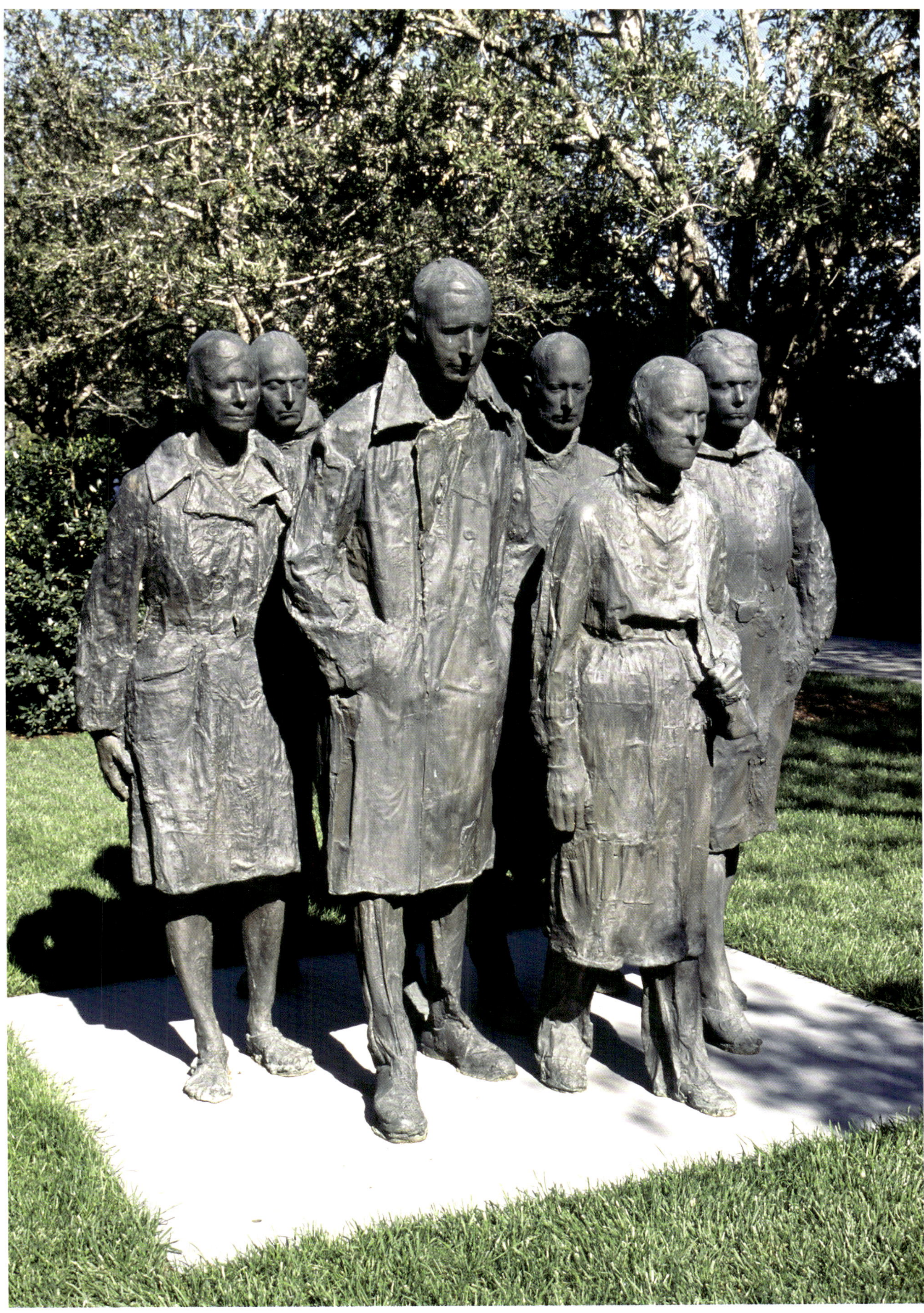

Installation of George Segal's
Depression Bread Line,
Washington, D.C., 1997

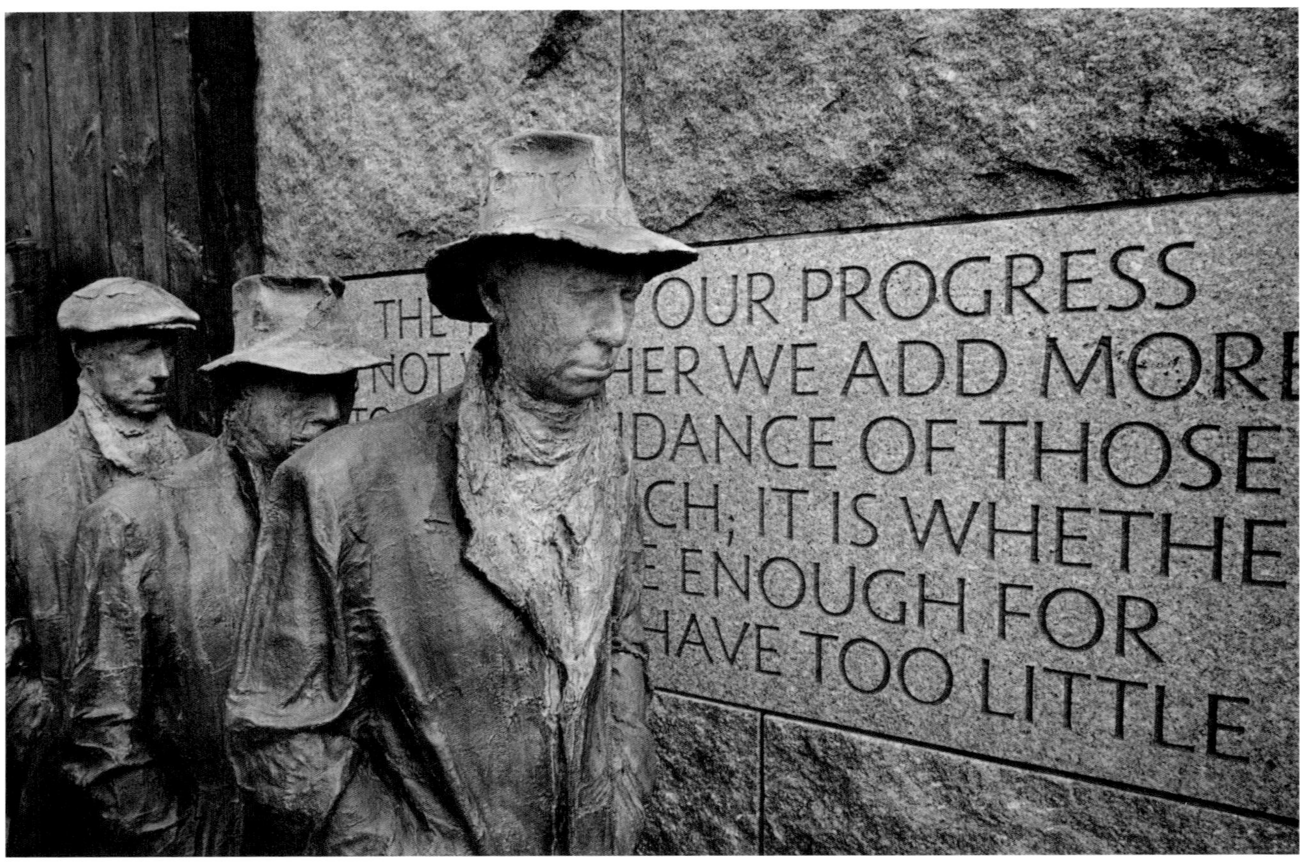

a theme and those he chose to pose for it. When he had an opening at the Janis Gallery, there were usually a few men and women around trying to appear nonchalant while stealing glances at plaster replicas of themselves. Sometimes, they would spot a fellow model across the room and smilingly make brief eye contact. I was in this privileged circle, having posed for George on two occasions. Though most of us had little idea who Segal's other models were—we could well have been figures in the same piece—we were a community. George had a way of bringing complete strangers together in his sculptures, making it seem as if they shared long histories.

Consider the down-and-outers in his 1991 *Depression Bread Line*, one of three bronze sculptures he was commissioned to make for the Franklin Delano Roosevelt Memorial, in Washington, D.C. (p. 18). A few years before commencing work on it, he told me about themes he had in mind. In addition to a line of destitute men, there would be an elderly Appalachian couple and a man intently listening to a Roosevelt fireside chat on an old Philco.

These pieces for the Roosevelt project would be drawn as much from his memories of those troubled times as from photographs and news coverage of that era. He immersed himself in the imagery of the 1930s, studying photographs by such master chroniclers as Walker Evans, Dorothea Lange, and Ben Shahn, the social realist painter who was also a perceptive photographer. Segal spoke with considerable feeling about hardships endured by his family, who, like other working-class people in dire straits, found hope in Roosevelt's words.

The more he talked about the bread line sculpture, the more I wanted to be part of it. So I dropped a few hints, and he got the message. When the casting call from South Brunswick finally came, I was ready.

The first Segal sculpture I posed for was the *Hot Dog Stand*, 1978, a depiction of a man about to buy a frankfurter from a bored-looking young woman, who, arms crossed, doesn't look at him (p. 19). Its inspiration was an actual stand Segal had come across in a New Jersey mall. What thrilled him about its discovery was its Mondrian-like ceiling, aglow with red, blue, yellow, and white rectangles. The ceiling he constructed in his studio was a duplicate of that in the mall. Though the ceiling is bright, its effect on the figures is not. The form of the young woman is distinct against the blackness of the stand she occupies, while my dark-painted double is well outside the area lighted from above. The *Hot Dog Stand*, for all the fidelity of its rendering, is more about ambiguity than the representation of some commonplace situation. Whatever was local about this theme vanished in George's interpretation of it.

It is this unsettling feeling and the subtle ways he achieved it that fill his sculptures with tension. Nothing in these scenarios is what it seems to be. Time is suspended and geography erased. However, given the specificity of the bread line sculpture he was planning and the prominent public site in Washington it was destined for, I thought that George would not

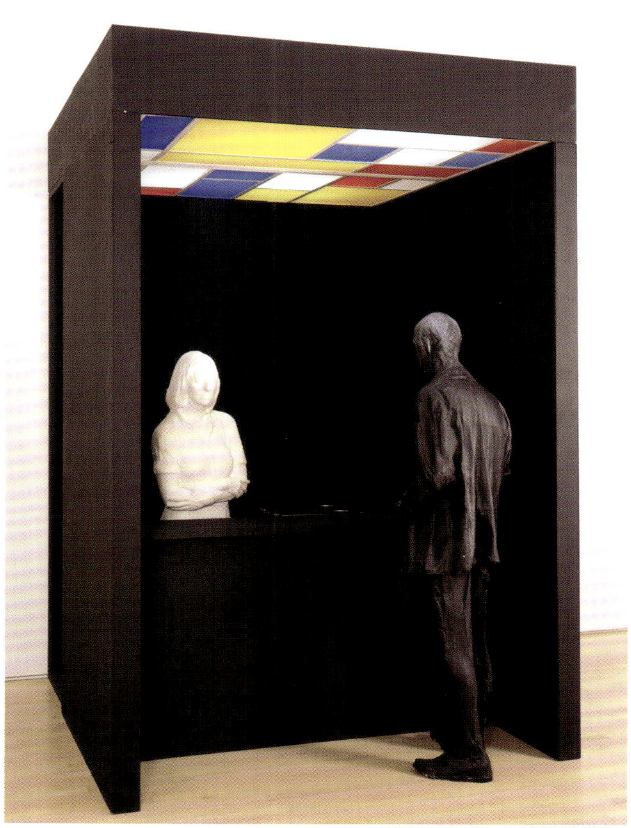

allow ambiguity to be so important a factor. After all, he would be telling a story in this and the other two sculptures about a stark period in American history. I thought they would be three-dimensional, matter-of-fact reportage, descriptive rather than allusive, and have in common a single theme: the consequences of poverty. I wondered how George could evoke that bleak era without overloading his sculptures with symbolic portent. And there was also the fact that commissioned sculptures were rarely his best works. I hoped the bread line would be an exception, which it turned out to be.

When, one summer day in 1991, I arrived at George's studio to take on my role of mendicant, three of the bread line's figures had been completed. There

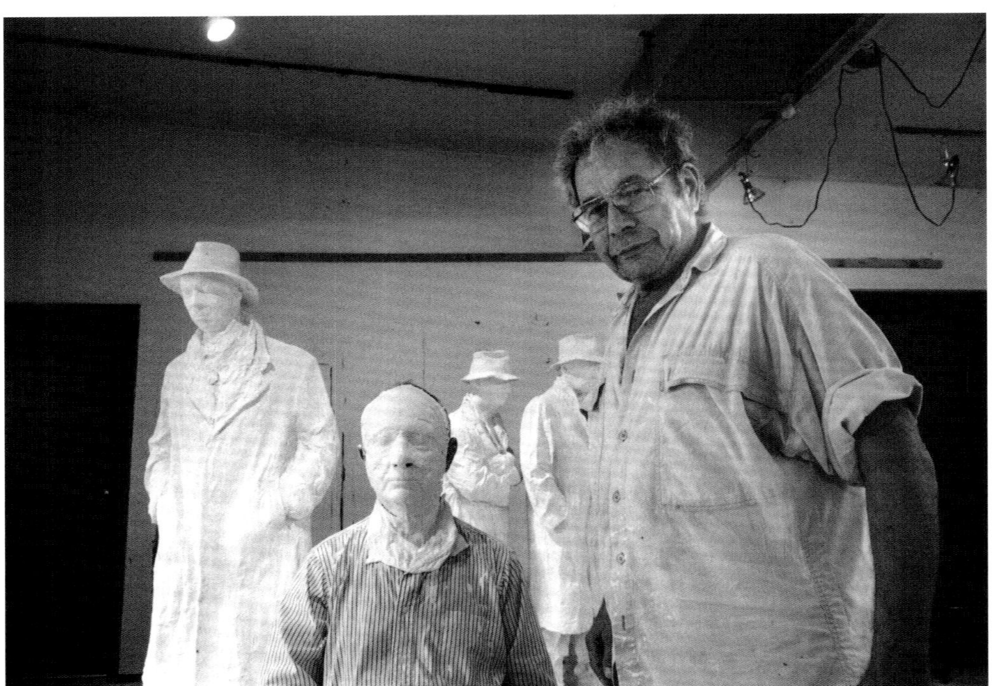

they stood, next to the casting area, waiting for me. One was Leon Bibel, a longtime artist friend, who lived near the Segals. Another was Donald Lokuta. The third completed was George himself, cast by Lokuta according to the master's instructions. Still to be made were representations of another Segal friend, Daniel Burger, who worked in the Metropolitan Museum's Mezzanine Gallery, and me. The recycled seedy overcoats and fedoras we wore were largely from local thrift shops.

George asked me to assume a comfortable pose. "Just stand still and look straight ahead," he said. What would I be looking at? The back of the man in front of me, he answered.

I had taken along a pair of chinos I was ready to sacrifice for the cause, knowing that they and the clothes he supplied were to be encased in wet plaster. Normally, Segal cast his models in three stages: first the torso, next the legs, and, finally, the head. As my borrowed overcoat extended to my knees, it became

part of the torso section. Once I had taken my stance, George traced the outline of my shoes in chalk on the studio's concrete floor so that I would be correctly positioned for the next phase, which consisted of casting my trousered legs and shoes. He also measured my height.

His low-tech process of replicating the body in plaster was governed as much by intuition as logic. It entailed completely covering the model in strips of plaster-impregnated Johnson & Johnson bandages, normally used for setting broken limbs. George and Lokuta worked speedily. Once the wrapping was complete, great gobs of wet plaster were slapped on my chest and back, which George proceeded to shape into ridges and valleys that loosely echoed my clothed body underneath. He emphasized the contours and folds of my finery, with special attention to the collar, sleeves, and shoulder seams. As my shell hardened, I grew increasingly warm, a comfortable feeling. An hour or so later, George gently pried it off. From my

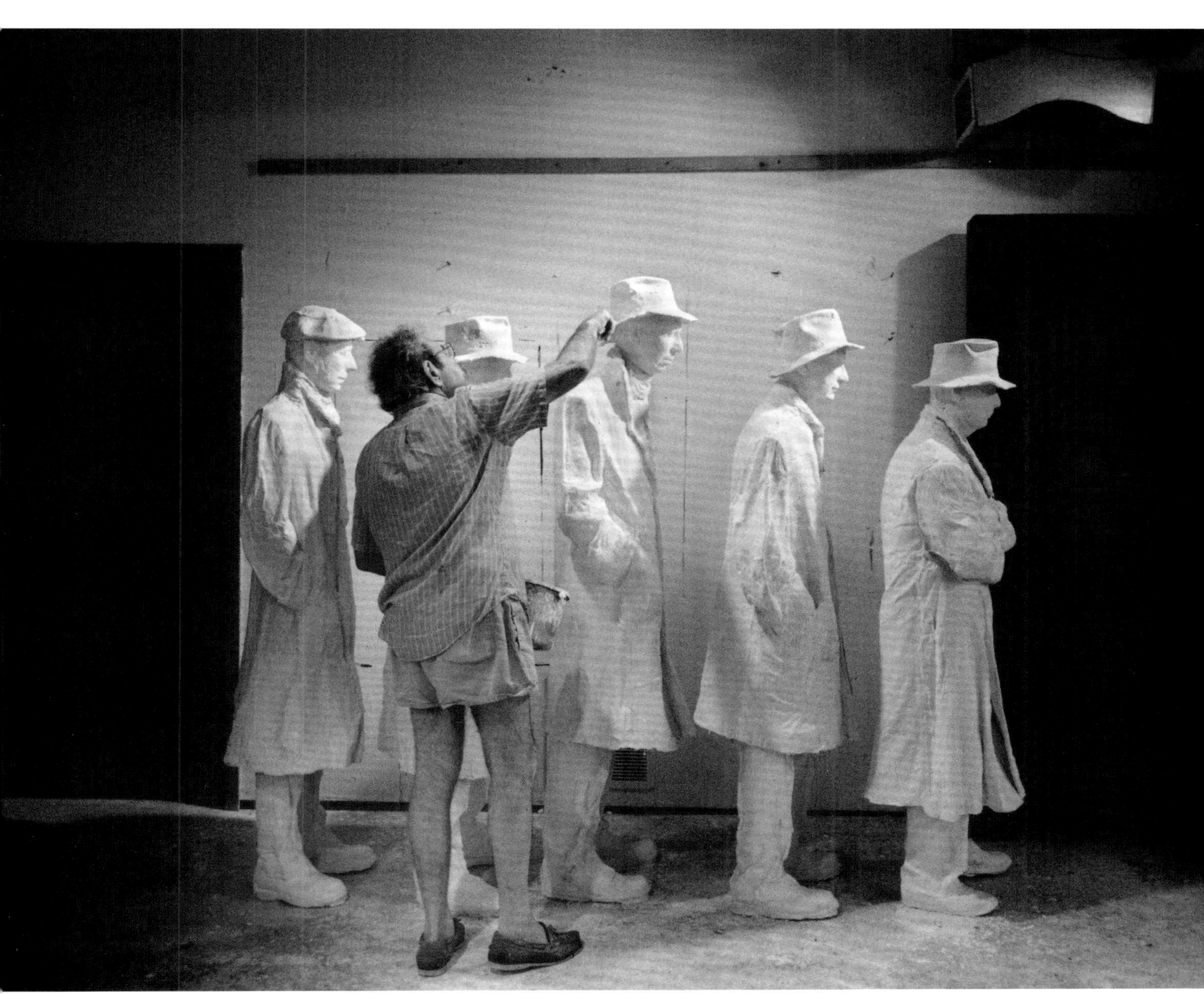

The artist completing
Depression Bread Line 1991
Subjects, from left: Daniel Burger,
George Segal, Donald Lokuta,
Martin Friedman, Leon Bibel

previous experience of being a Segal model, I knew the best part was to come.

When it was time to cast my head, I would be able to sit for a while and listen to music, however faintly the sound came through my plaster cocoon. After a liberal application of Nivea, a lubricant cream, to my eyelashes and eyebrows, George swathed my head in layers of wet cloth. He told me to take a deep breath and forcefully let it out through my nose to make a breathing hole. As the plaster hardened, my head felt as though it were in an eggshell, a rather thick one. What a fine way to lose track of time and place, I thought. So much had I enjoyed the experience that I was reluctant to part with my shell when George tapped me on the head to let me know the time had come. Then he delicately pried it off. My eyelashes and eyebrows, I was glad to learn, were still intact. I was aware that my features would be reconstituted in white plaster, along with the rest of me, when George later filled these molds with liquid plaster after I had left the studio. There was a pile of plaster shells of body parts on the studio floor that he had peeled off other models. I wondered how he could pick his way through these, and which torso went with which set of legs.

Once my figure had emerged from its molds, George applied a few finishing touches of wet plaster, smoothing junctions between limbs and working over its surface lightly. He then positioned all five figures in a row. That decision taken care of, he set about painting them, using a deep green acrylic through which the white plaster beneath glowed. He covered the plaster impression of the brick wall they stood in front of with the same luminous color.

On May 1, 1992, the Sidney Janis Gallery opened an exhibition of the plasters for Segal's sculptures for the FDR Memorial. It was there that I had my first look at my plaster double. He was a little taller than I am, but we shared a slouched posture. I had trouble connecting with him, because he was more part of the group than an individual.

After the Janis exhibition, George had the plasters for his three FDR Memorial pieces transported to the Johnson Atelier in Mercerville, New Jersey, north of Trenton, for translation into bronze. Once that alchemy had been performed in the Atelier's foundry, he enthusiastically took on the job of patinating his newly minted bronze people. He went about this as if he were making a painting. The Atelier's technicians had applied a matte black undercoat to each piece to serve as grounds for his brushwork. In one hand he held a pastry brush—not an artist's brush—that he periodically dipped into the patinating mixture. In the other he held an acetylene torch. He alternately brushed and spattered the viscous, dark-green patinating solution onto each figure, then heated each worked-over area with the torch, thus binding the patina to the sculpture's surface. The mixture ran in rivulets, filling crevices in the bronze. The effect was that of bronze long exposed to the elements.

The bronze version of the bread line, along with the other two Segal sculptures for the FDR Memorial, was to be part of a seven-and-a-half-acre complex designed by the landscape architect Lawrence Halprin. Segal was one of five artists Halprin had selected. The others were Leonard Baskin, Neil Estern, Robert Graham, and Tom Hardy. Of them, the most

prominent were Baskin, known for his richly
expressionistic drawings, and Graham, best known for
his idealized male and female nudes. Separating the
Memorial's four roofless, roomlike sectors were
massive walls of stone and mini-waterfalls. How any-
thing so complex and stylistically varied got built
remains a question. In my less-than-objective opinion,
the trio of Segal sculptures is the most accessible,
Depression Bread Line the most affecting. This
procession of figures stands outside a mysterious door,
in limbo. Something other than attire and their
shadowy blackish-green tonality unites them. They
share an emotional bond.

On May 2, 1997, the Franklin Delano Roosevelt
Memorial in West Potomac Park, on the edge of the
Tidal Basin, was dedicated. A year later, George
and I happened to be in Washington at the same time
and visited the Memorial together. The day was brisk
and wintry, and the figures in the line seemed dressed
appropriately in their shabby overcoats. I quickly
spotted my slightly stooped alter ego behind the figure
of Leon Bibel. I had mixed feelings upon seeing him
there. True, he looked like me, but I felt even less
identification with this version than the plaster one.
Perhaps it was because of the overwhelmingly official
context of the Memorial itself, with its overload of
entablatures and insignia commemorating Roosevelt's
presidency. The bread line had a compelling intimacy.
At the same time, though, it assumed a mythic
dimension. My companions and I stand in perpetuity,
outside a closed door. The door, part of the brick
wall behind the figures, is a mystery. On one hand it
is that of a soup kitchen, on the other a possible

entrance to oblivion. Thus, once again George had it
both ways—a description of an everyday event, but one
that took on universal meaning. Indeed, there is an
indeterminancy about this sculpture despite the
immediacy of its subject matter. Poverty is clearly the
theme. Static as this composition may seem, it emits
an unsettling energy. The figures' richly textured
surfaces—the residual traces of George's hand-shaping
process—vary dramatically under changing light
conditions. Dark, indistinct areas were illuminated
during the brief periods of sunshine on that otherwise
bleak day. Interdependent as the figures are, each
man looks inward. The evidence of the artist's hand
is everywhere. I'm glad George kept a place in line
for me.

*Note: Parts of this article are
drawn from pieces the author has
written about George Segal
for* Art in America *magazine and*
Sculpture *magazine.*

George Segal
Street Scenes

Cinema 1963

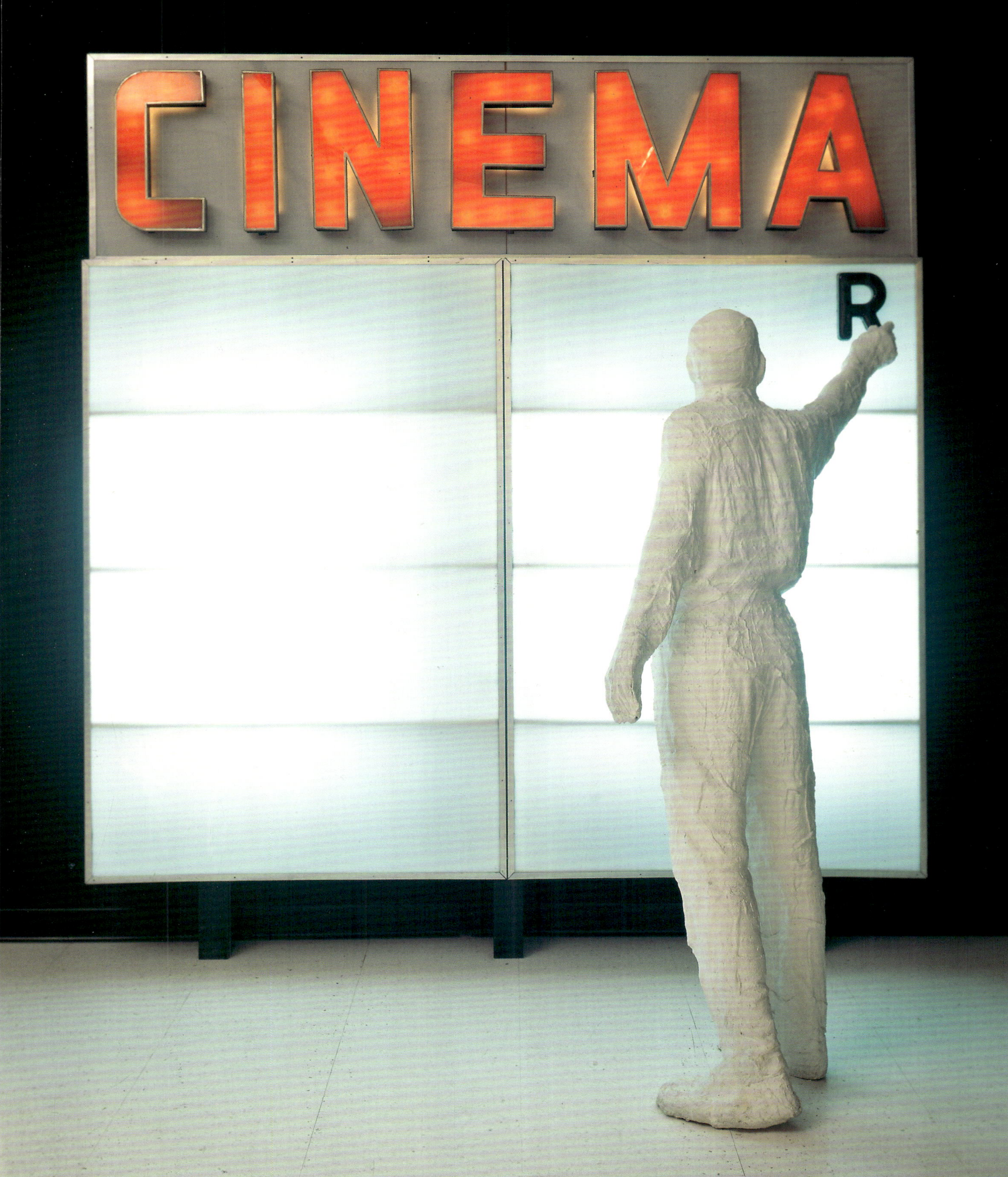

CINEMA
R

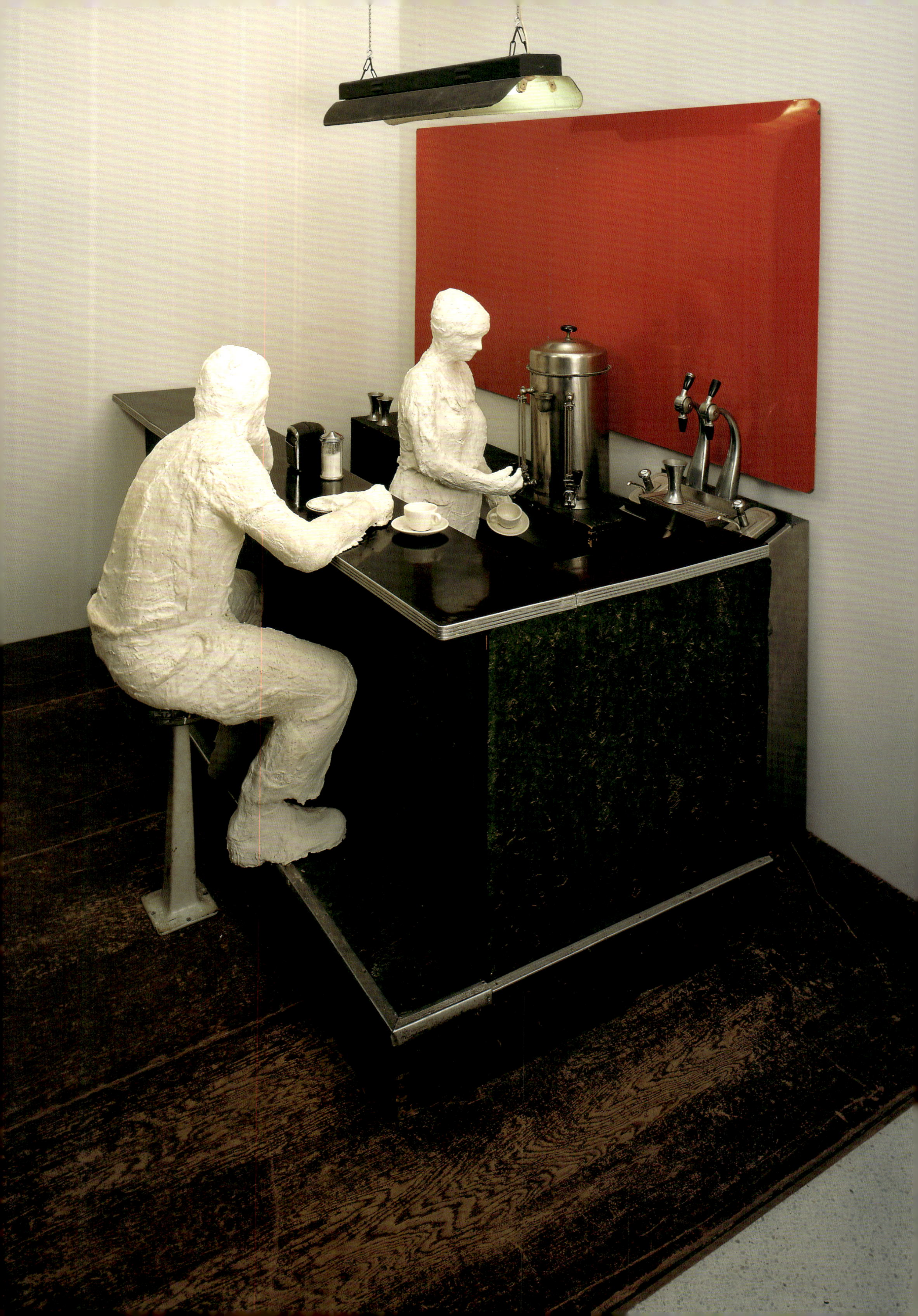

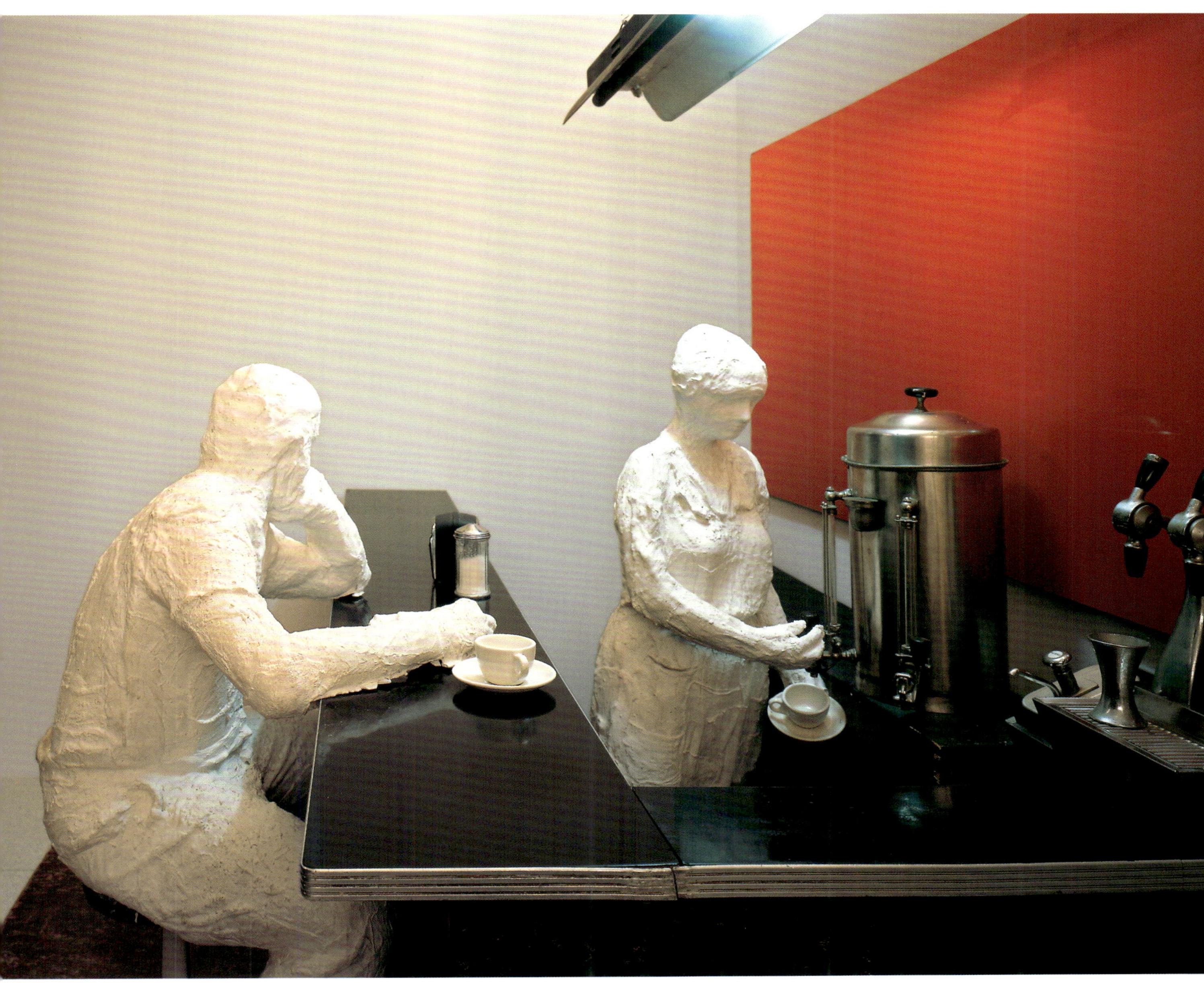

Girl in Doorway I 1965

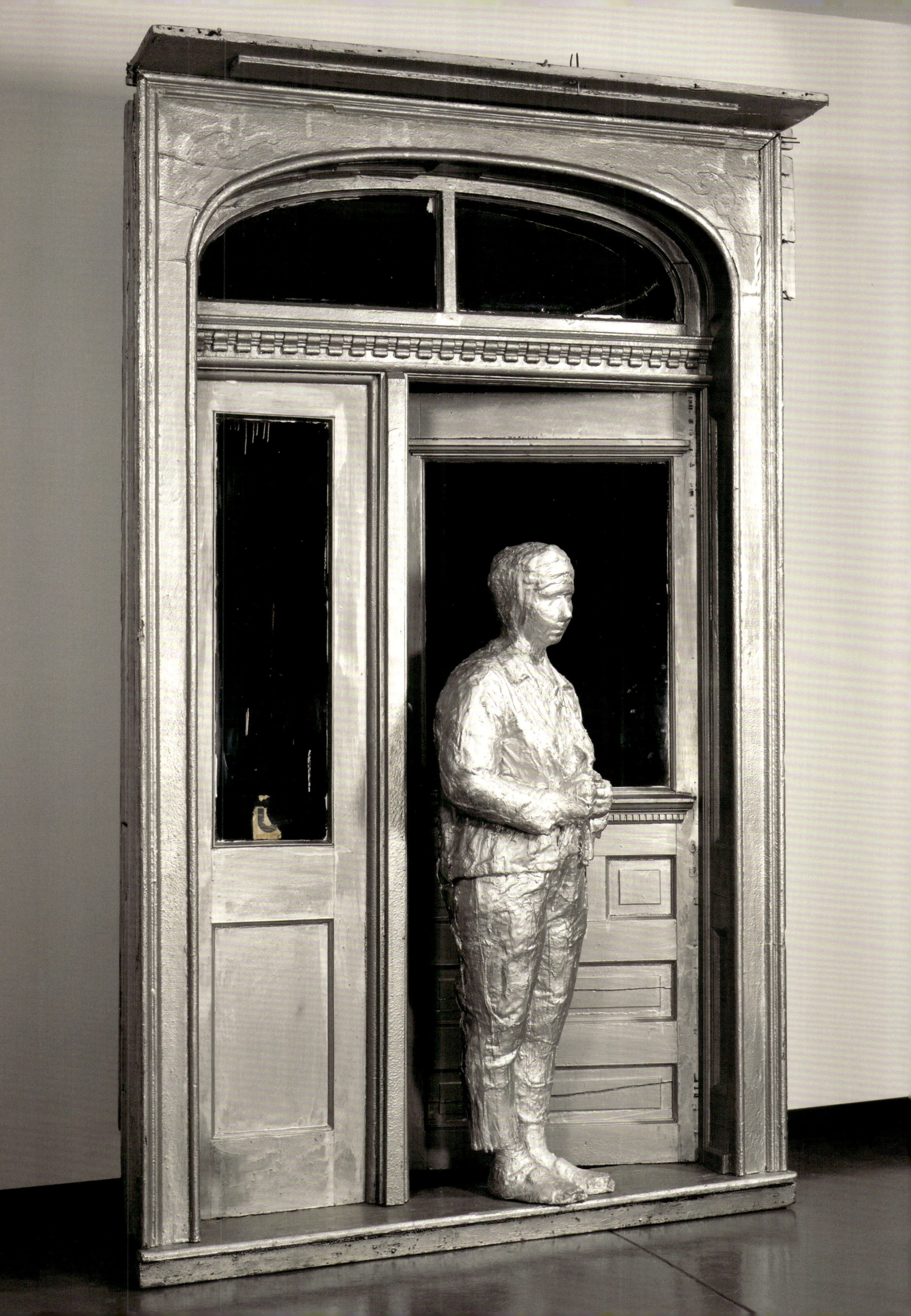

The Parking Garage 1968

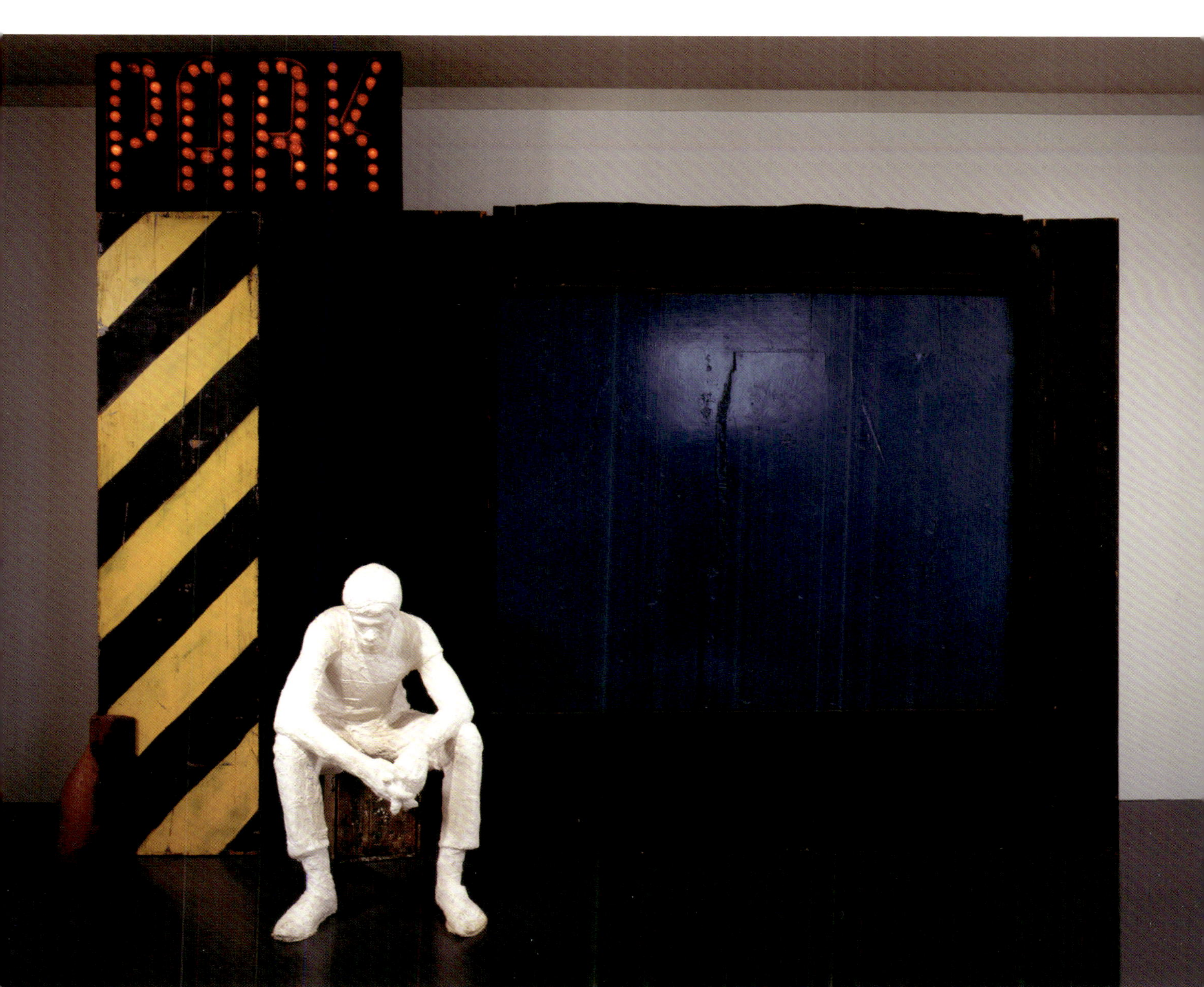
PARK

Box: Man in a Bar 1969

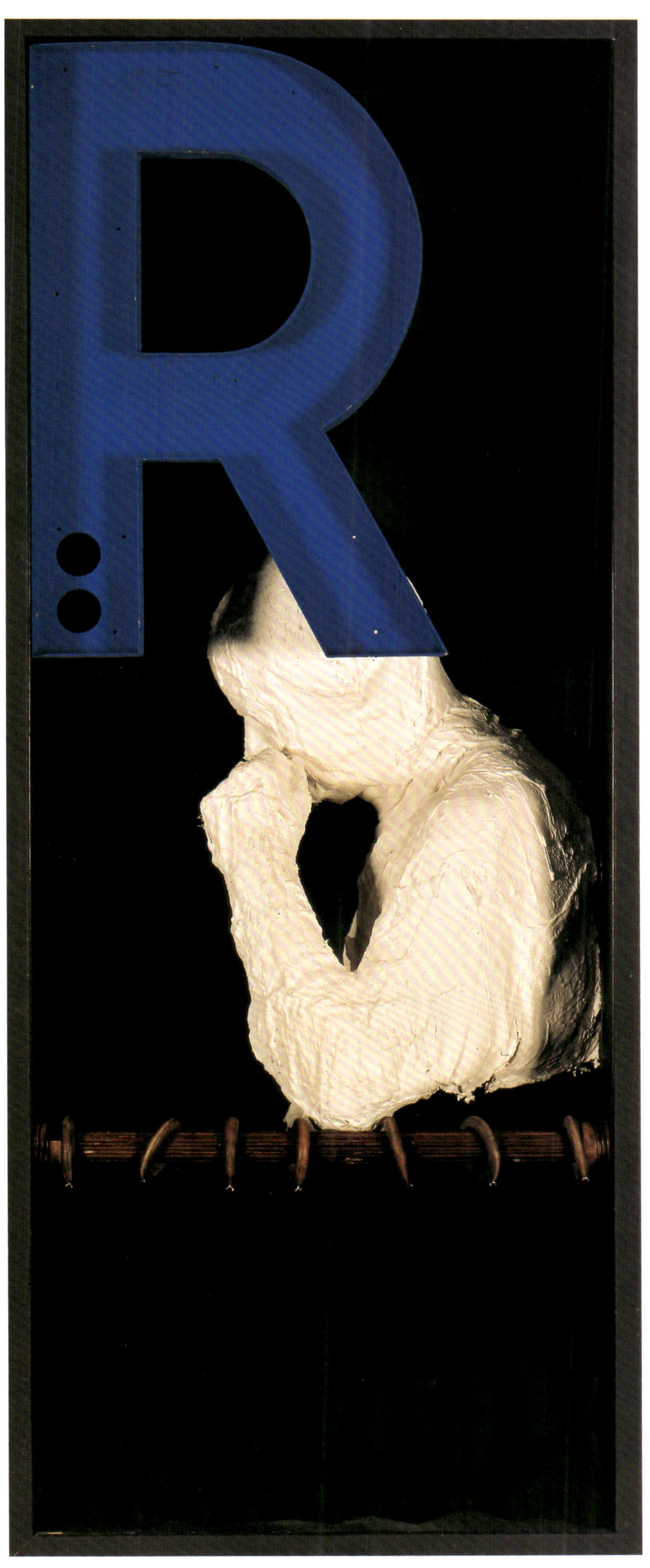
R

Japanese Couple against Brick Wall 1981

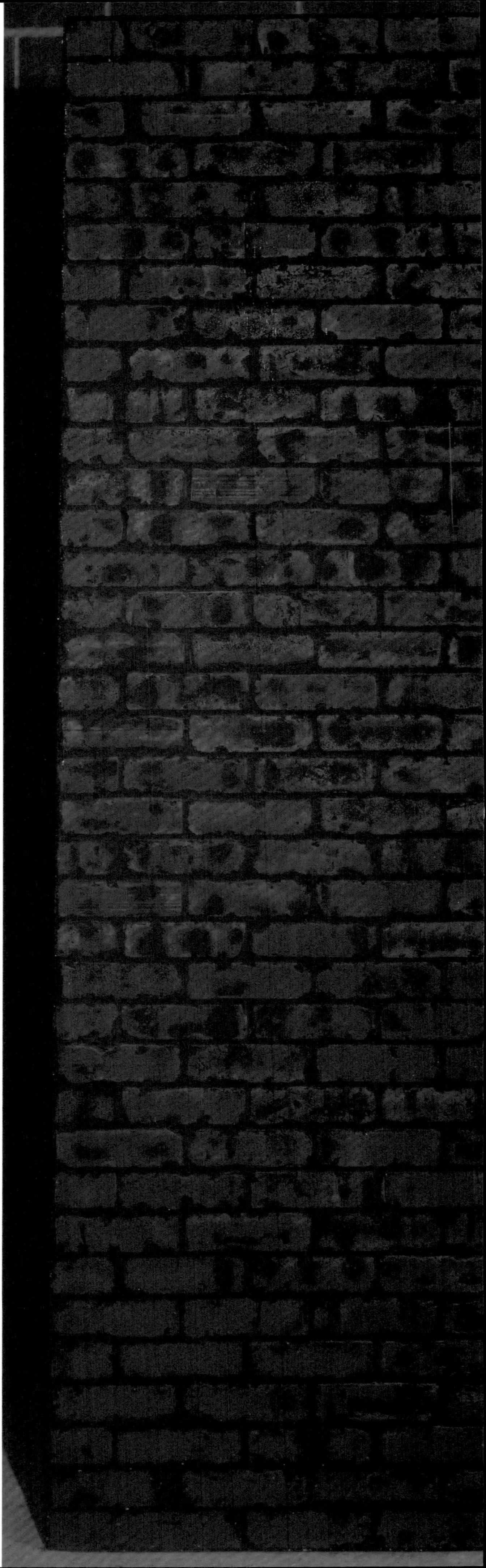

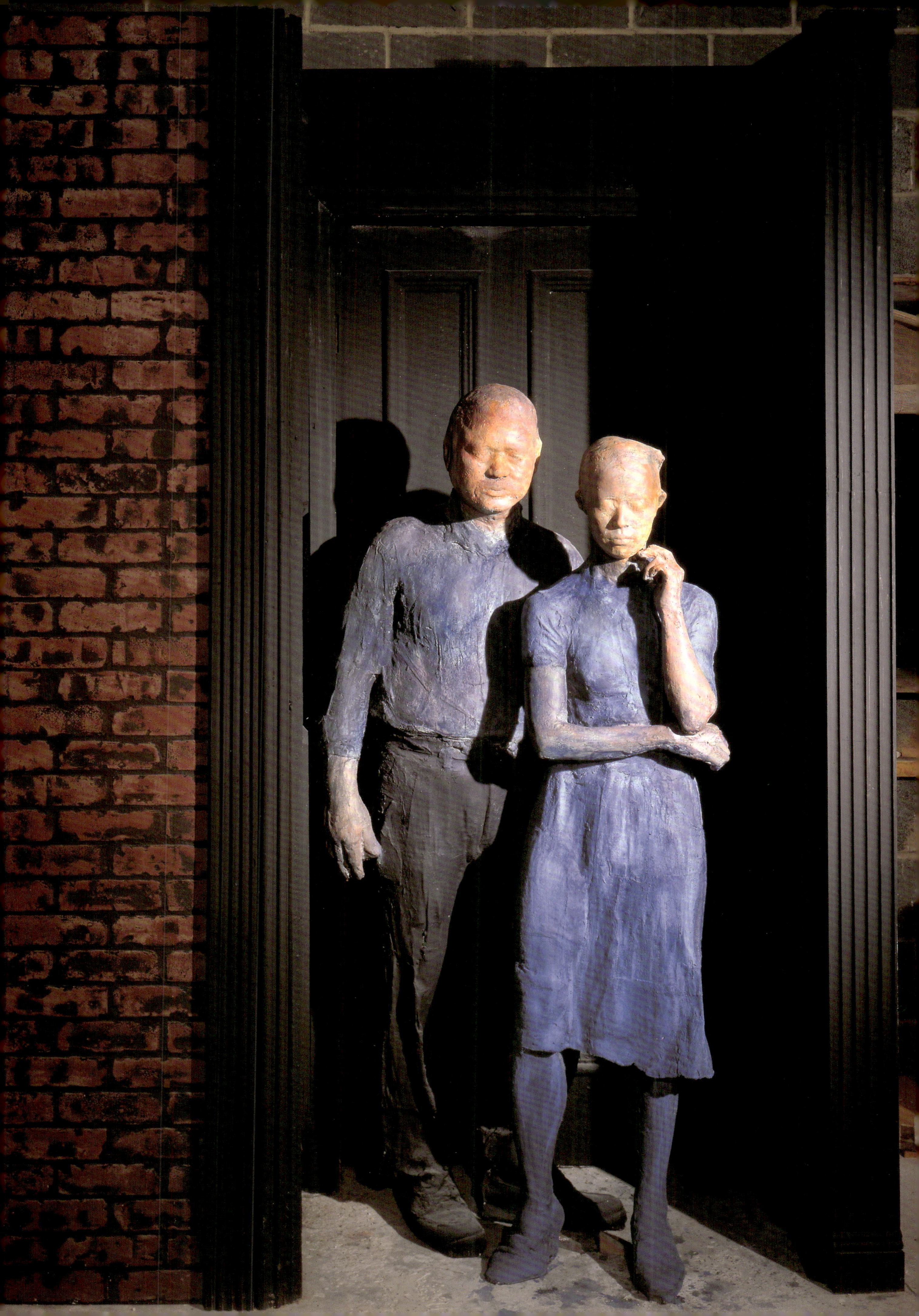

Restaurant Diner Still Life 1983

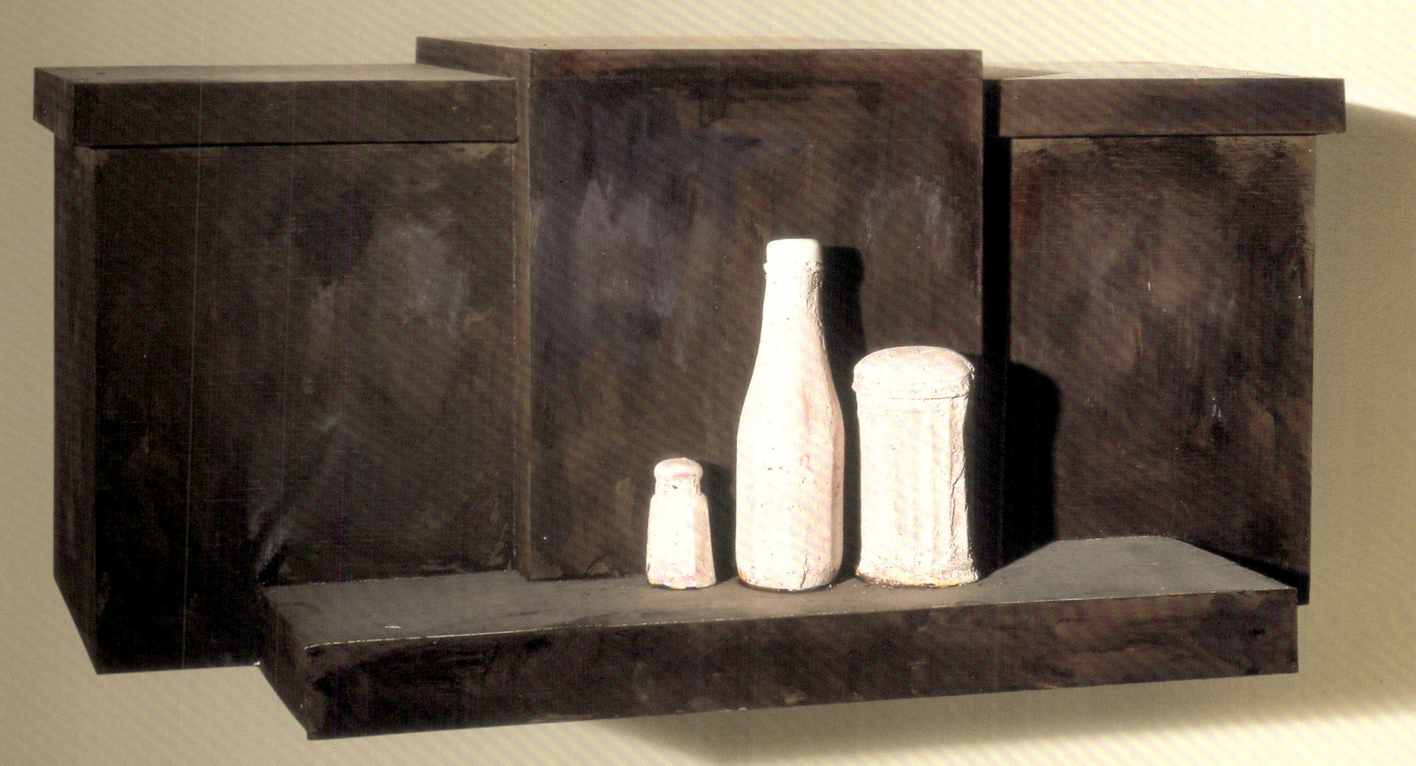

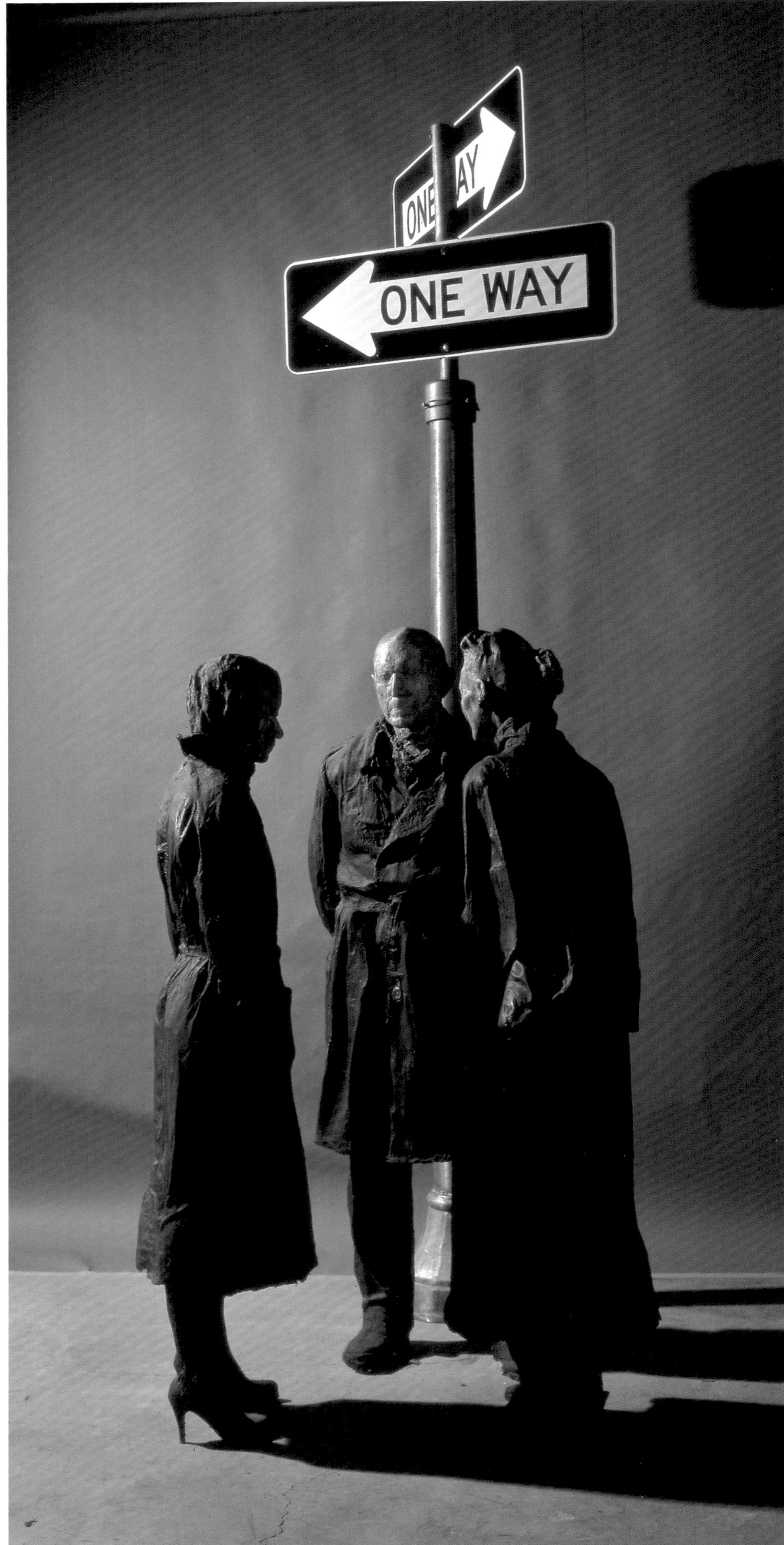

Chance Meeting 1989

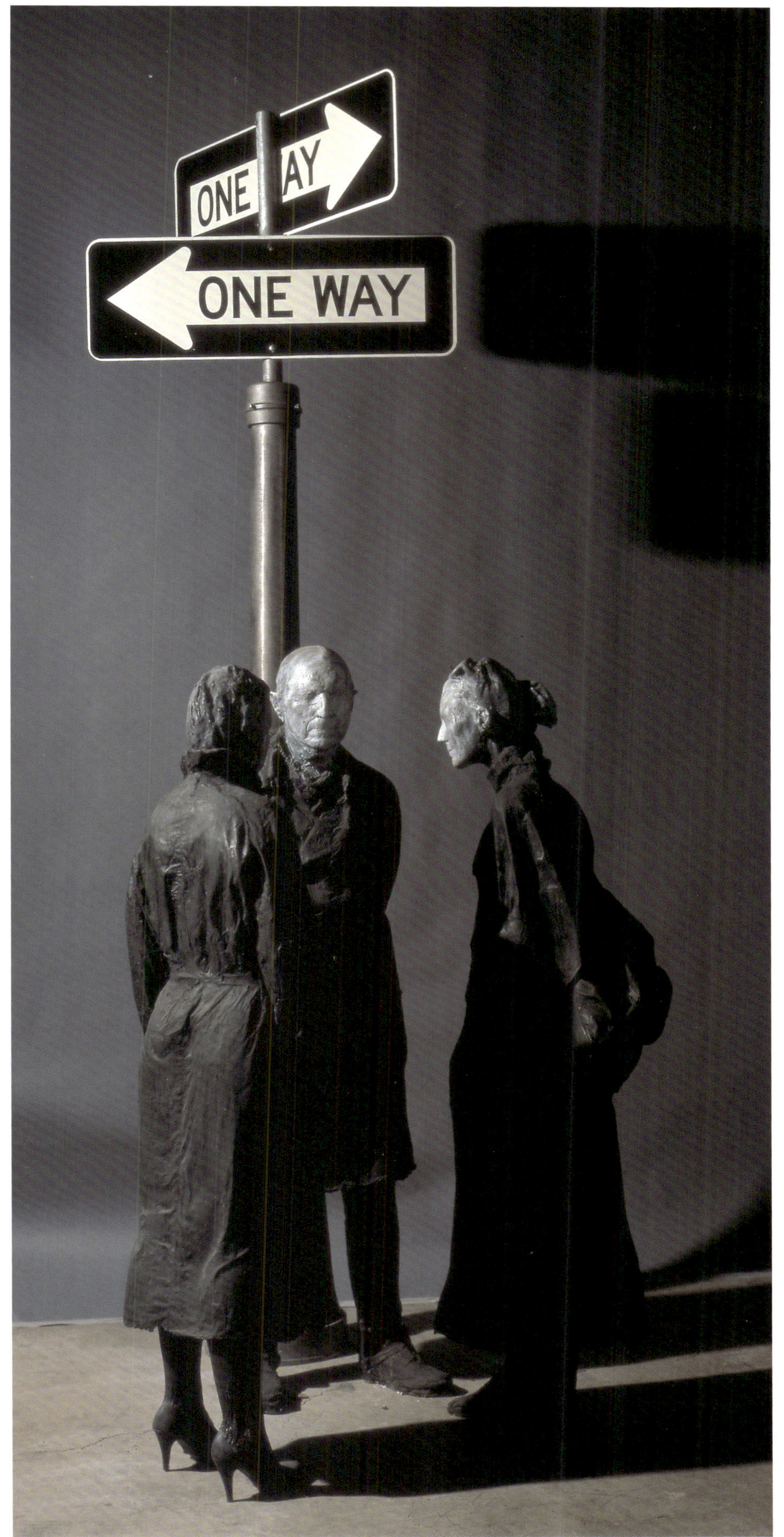

The Homeless 1989
pp. 40–41

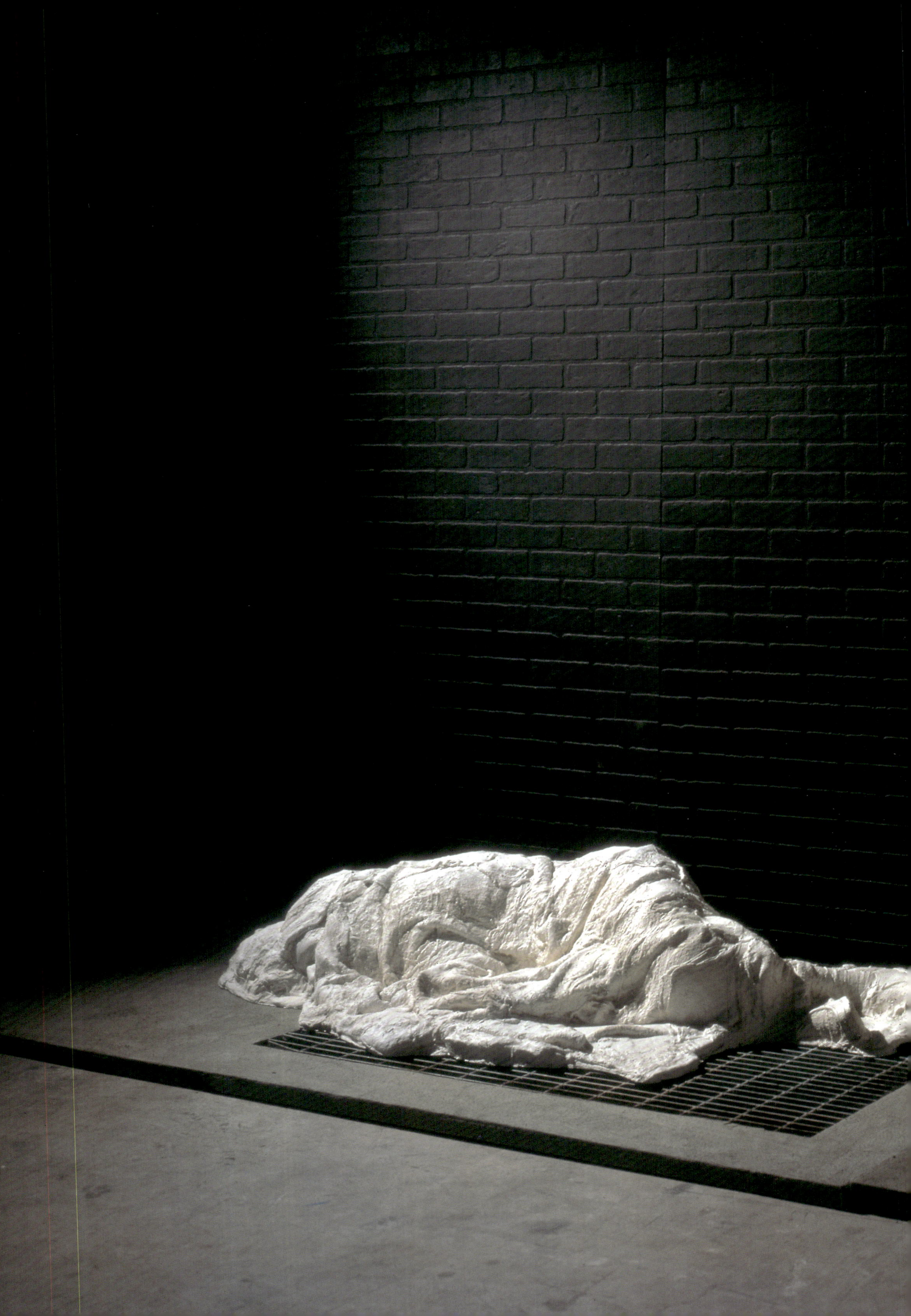

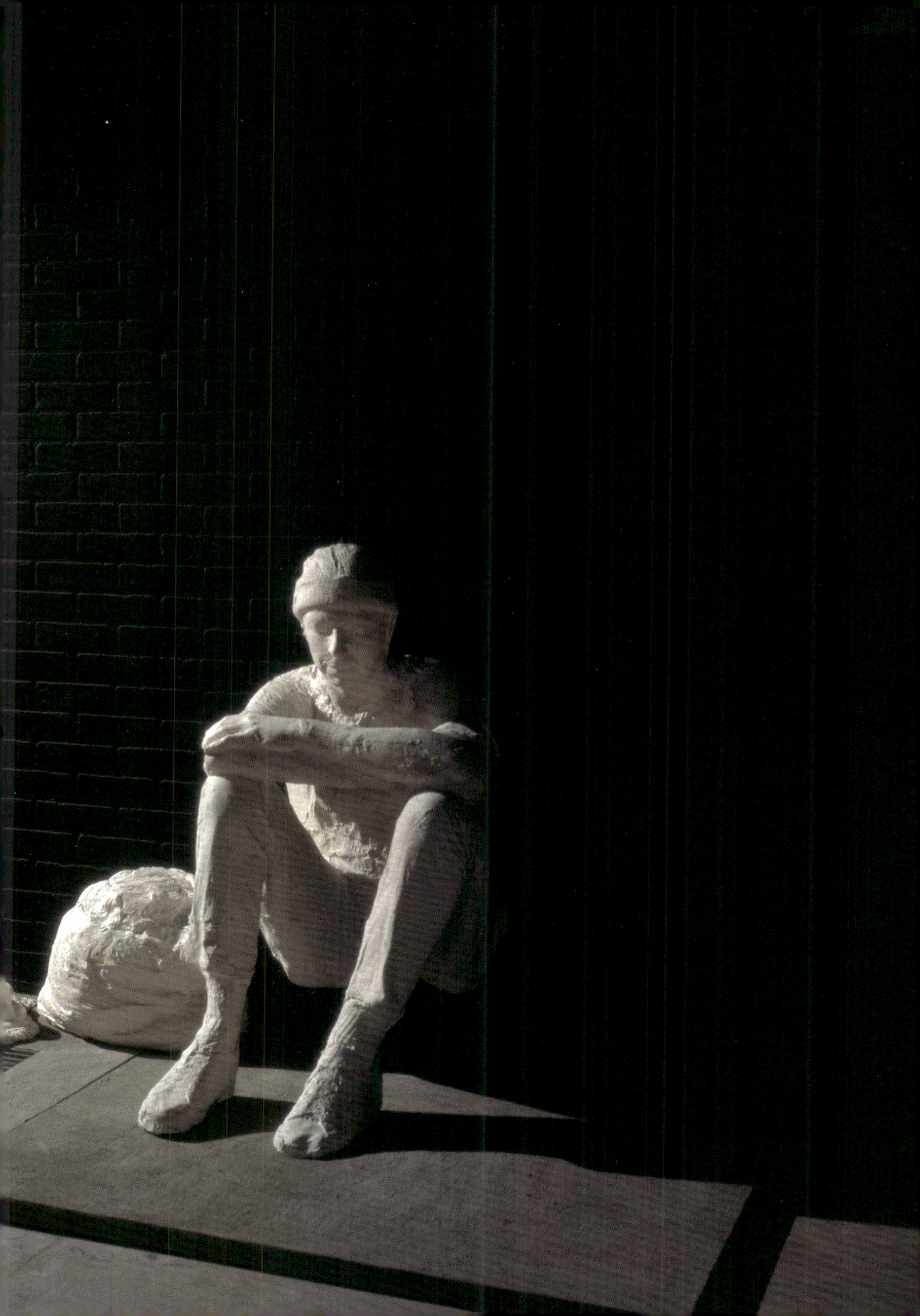

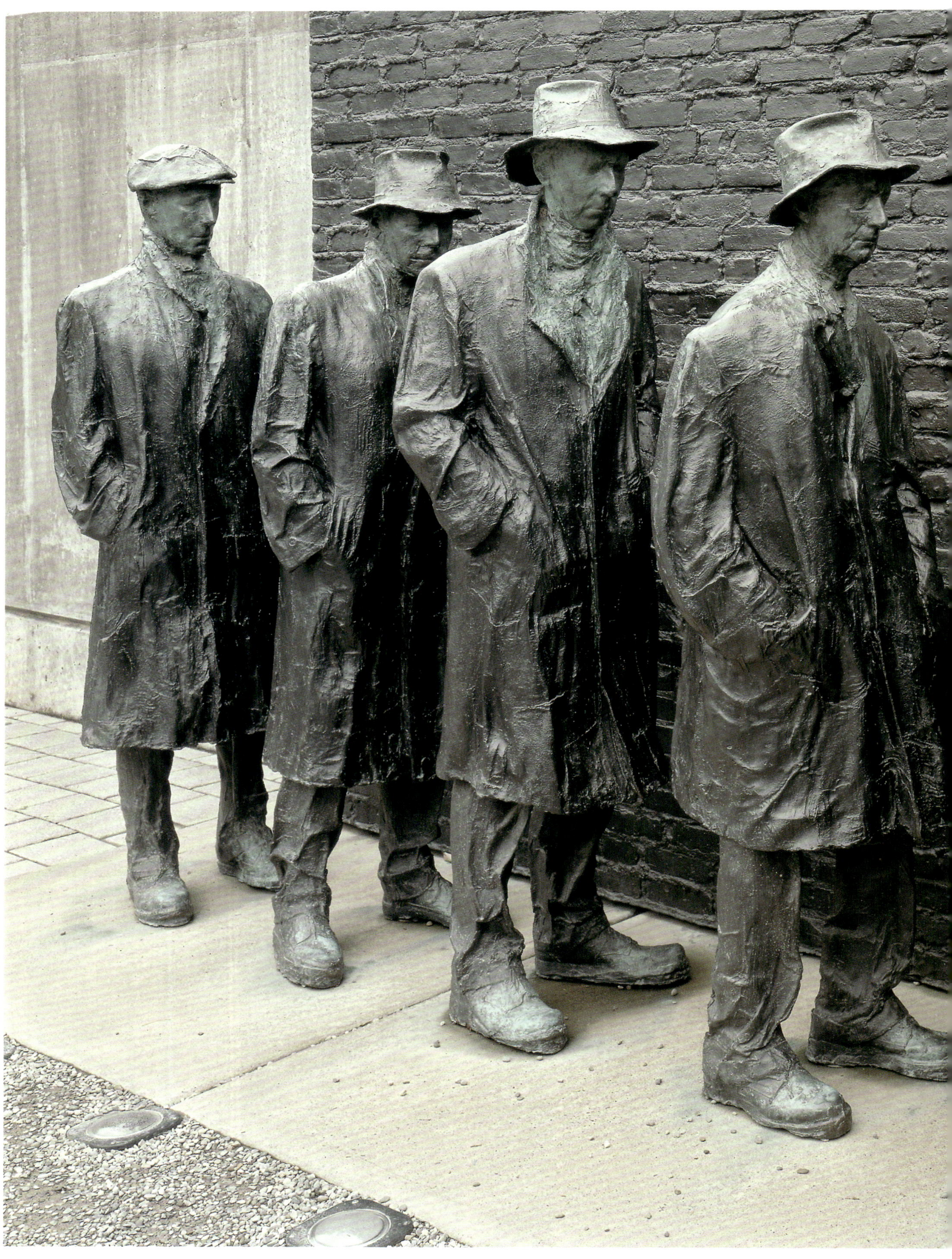

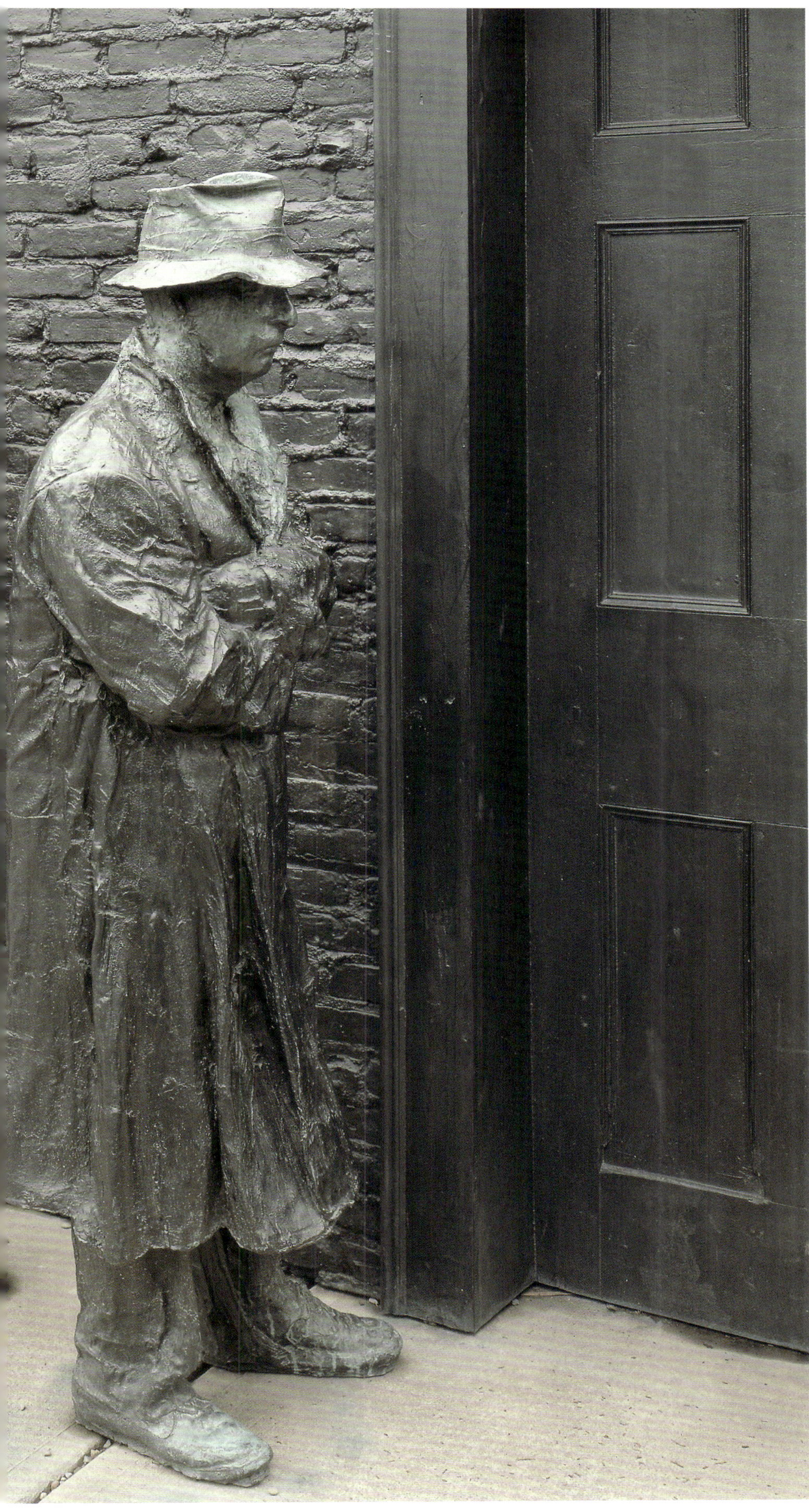

Depression Bread Line
1991

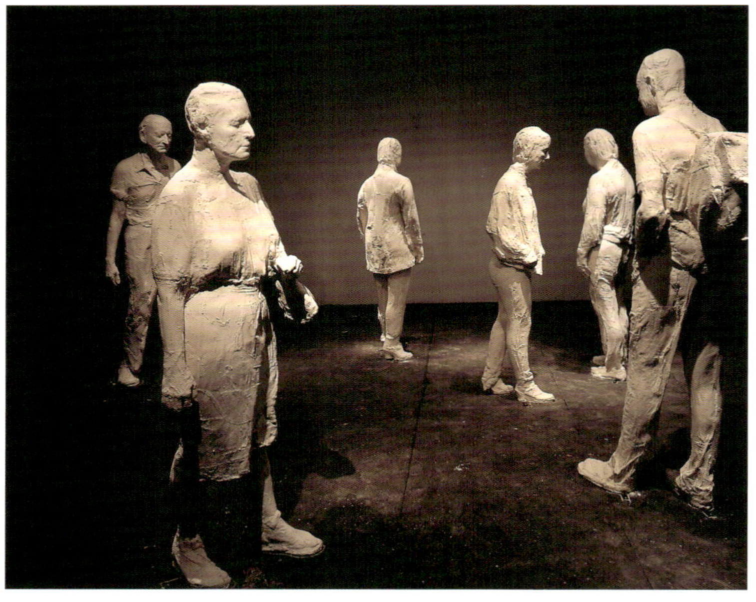

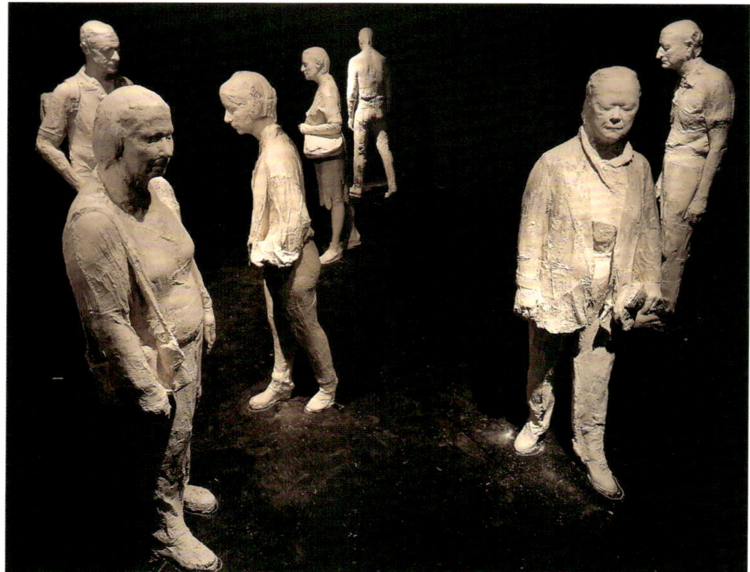

Street Crossing 1992

(four views)

44

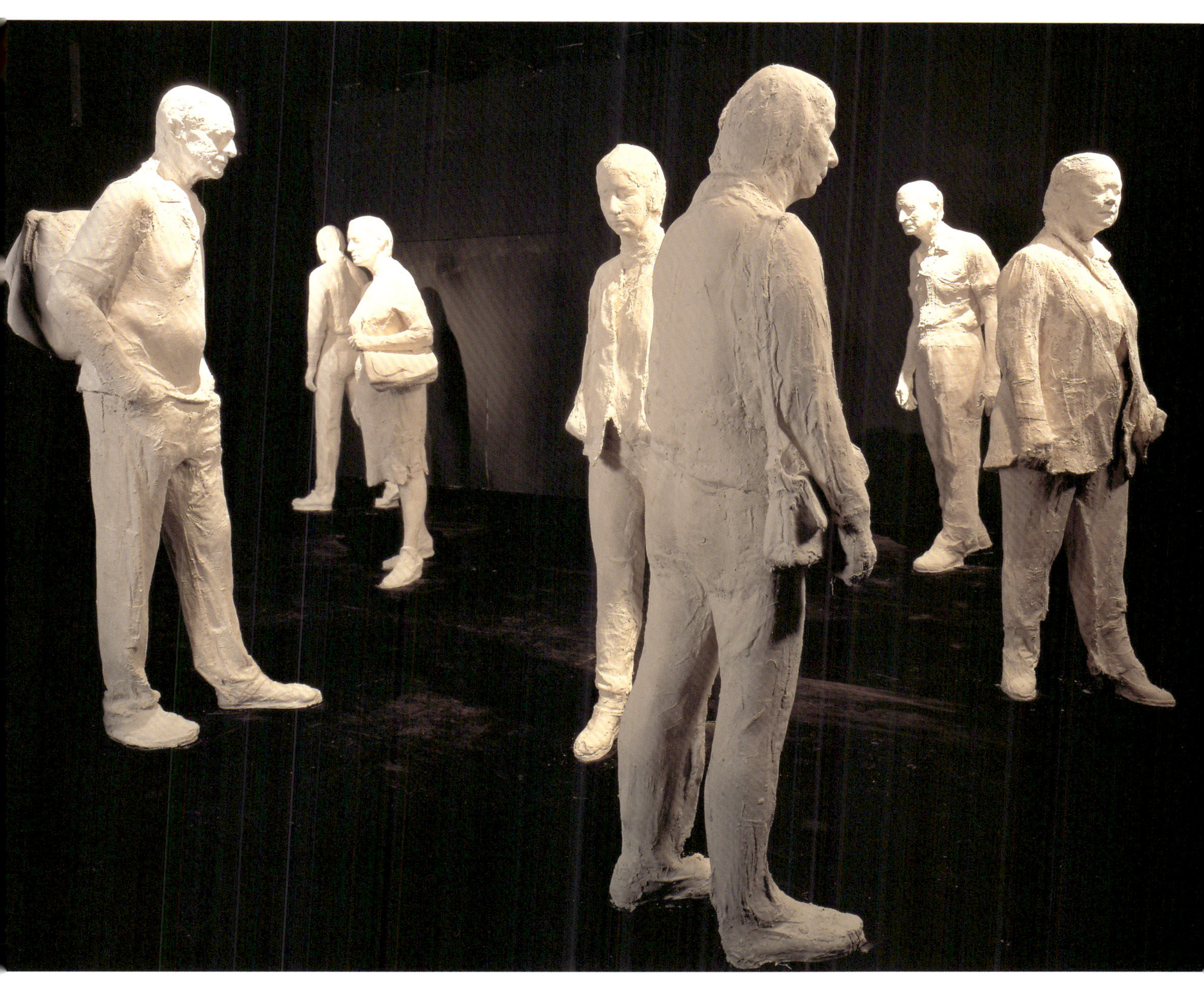

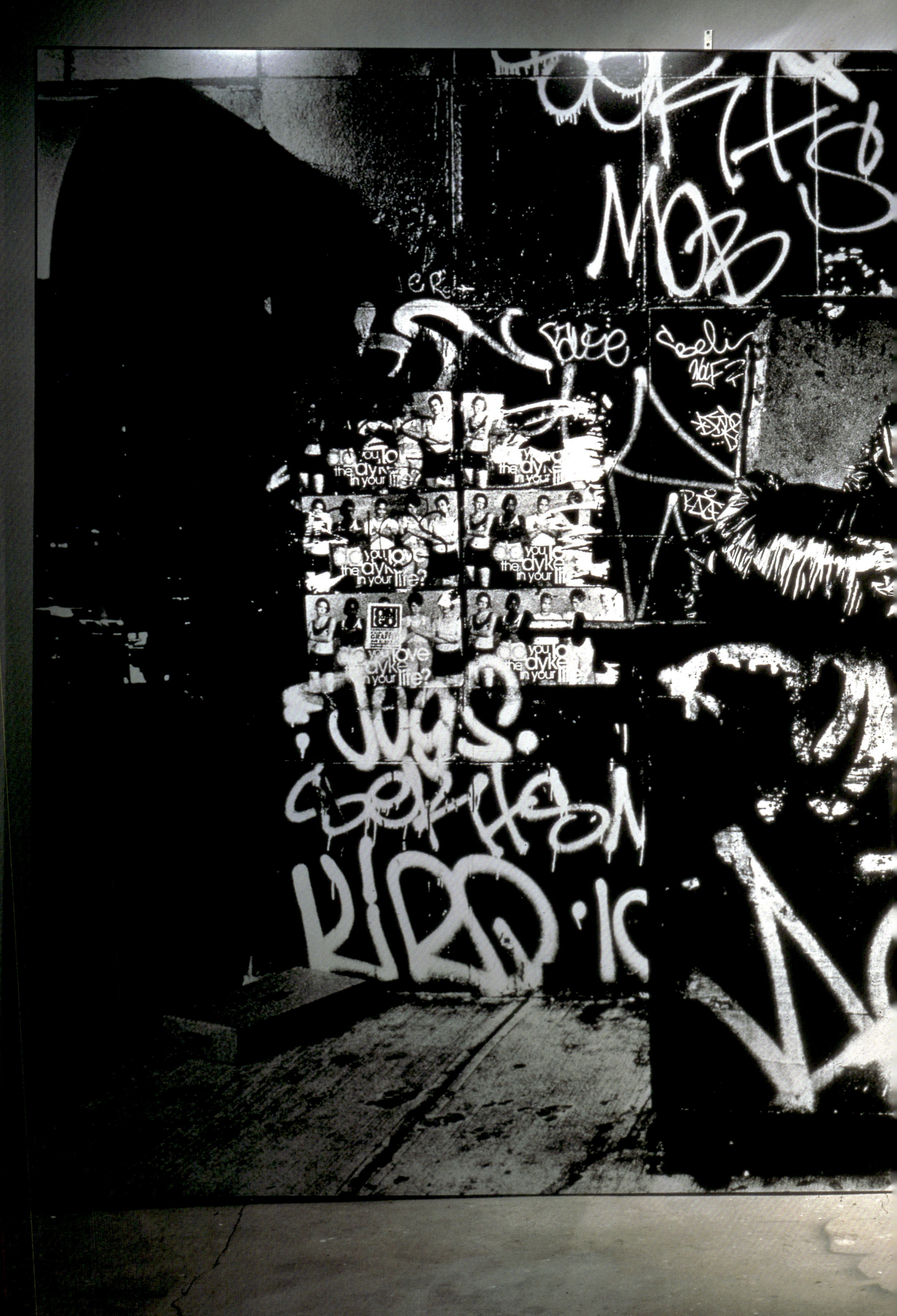
are you love
the dyke
in your life?
JUGS.

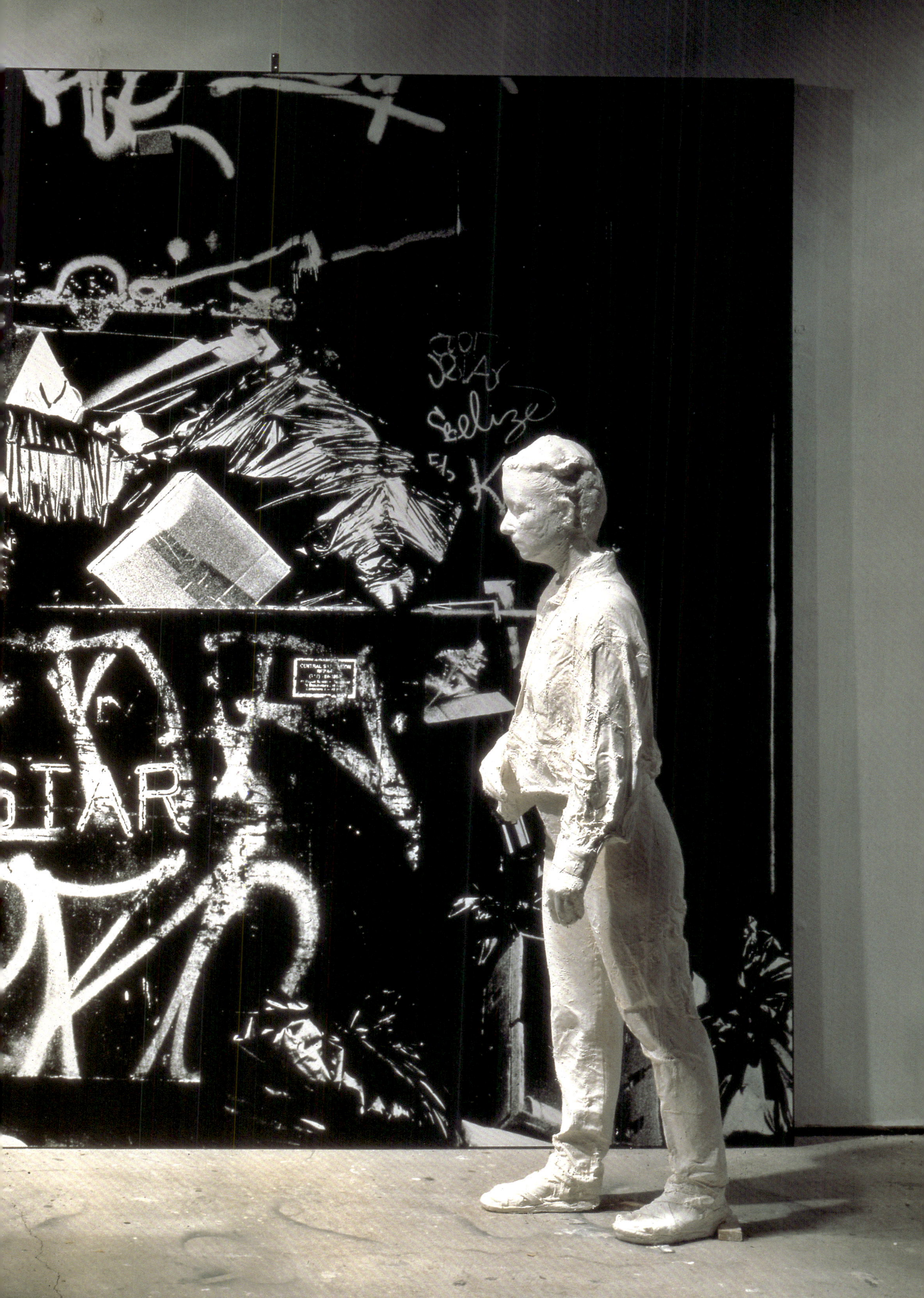
STAR

Liquor Store 1994

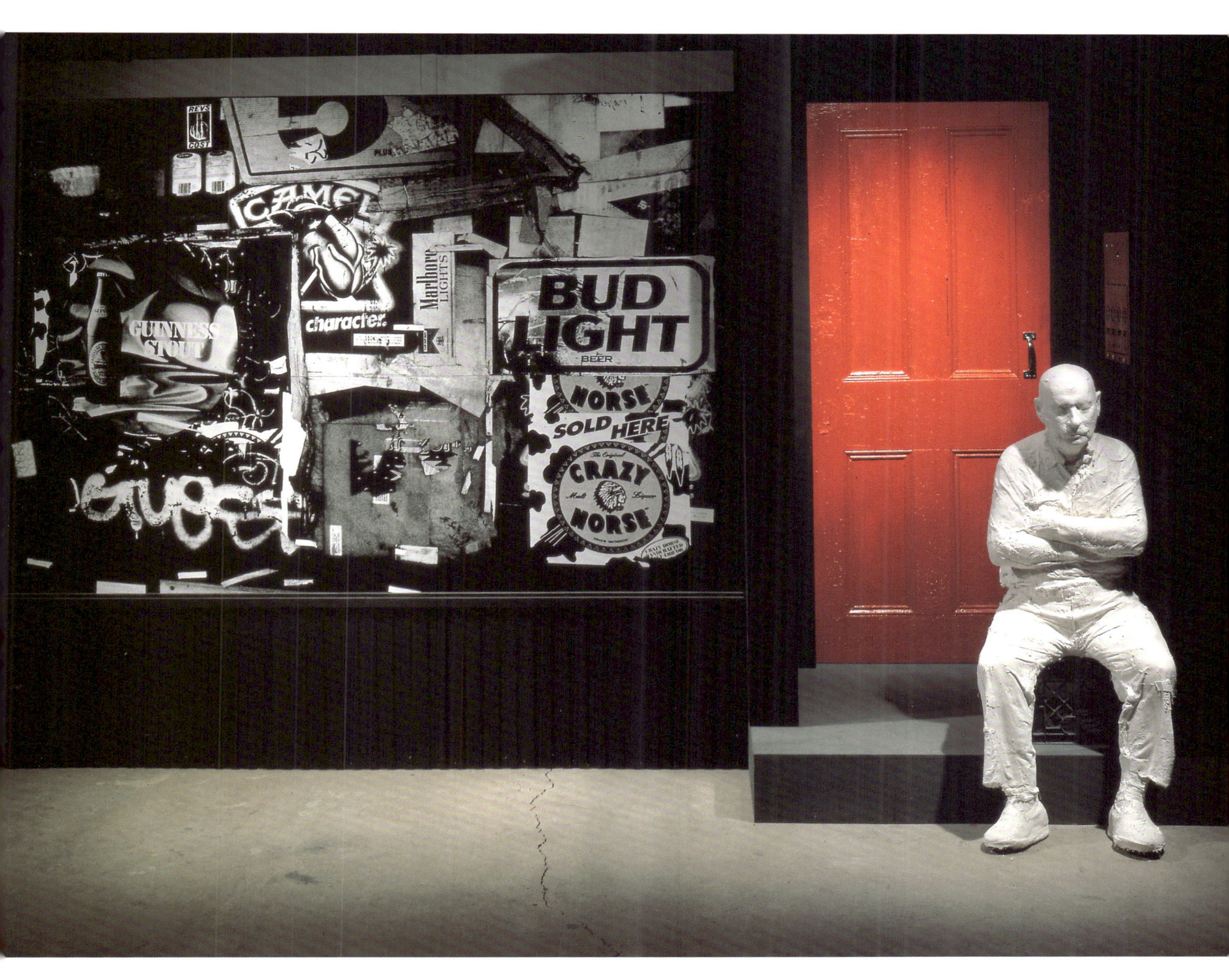
REV'S
COST
CAMEL
GUINNESS
STOUT
Marlboro LIGHTS
character.
BUD
LIGHT
BEER
HORSE
SOLD HERE
CRAZY
HORSE

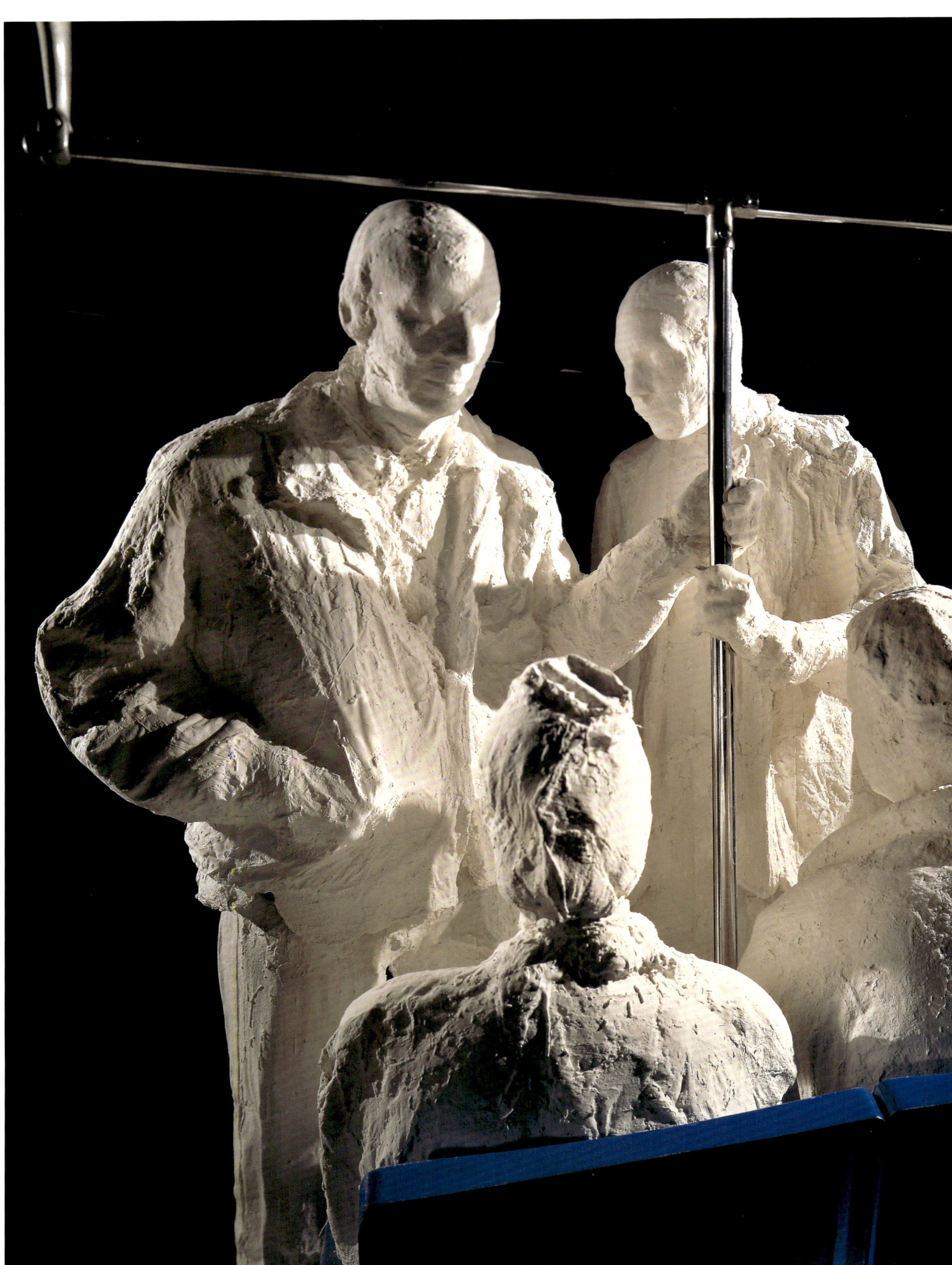

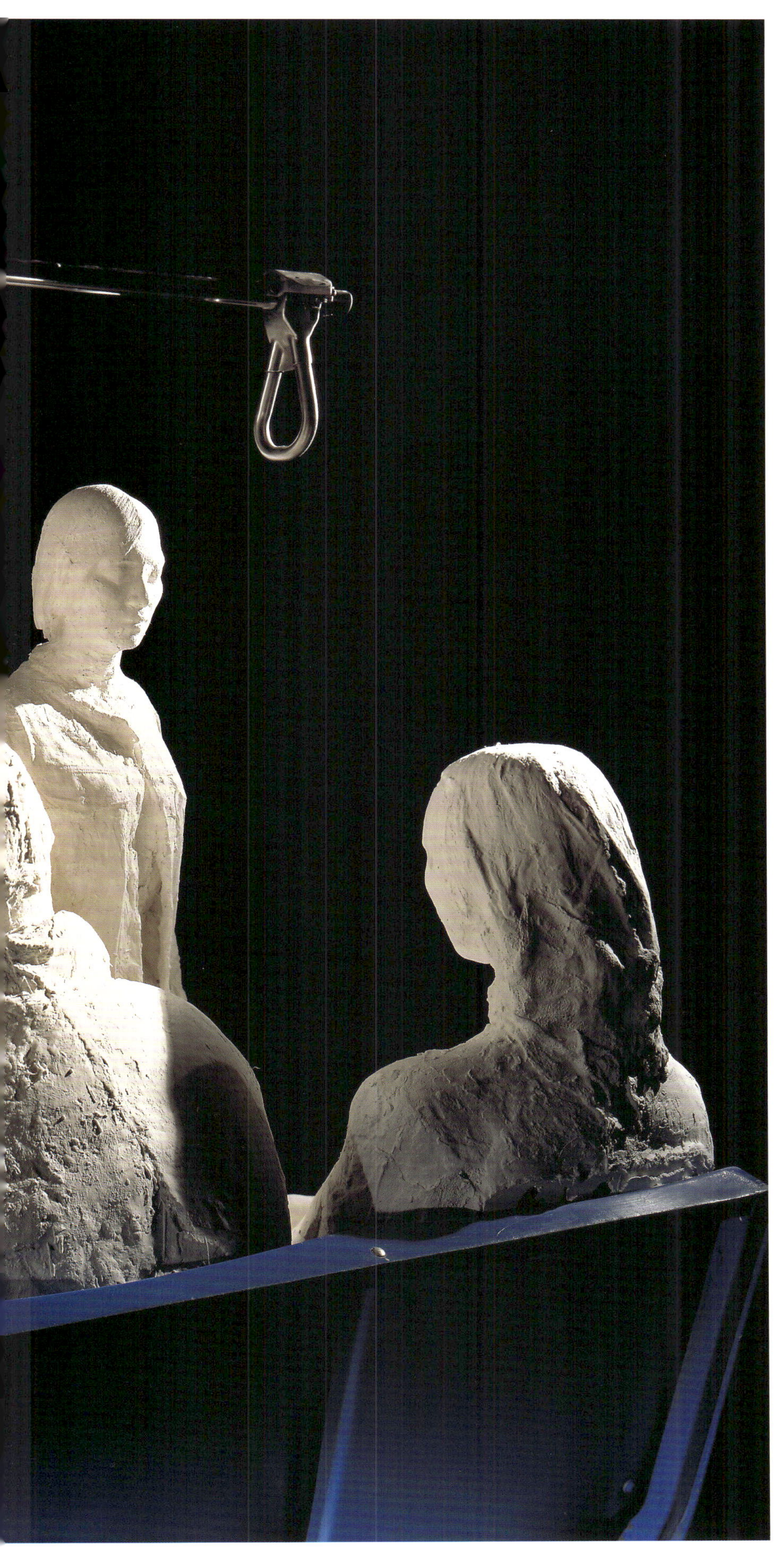

Bus Passengers 1997

Woman on the Bench 1997

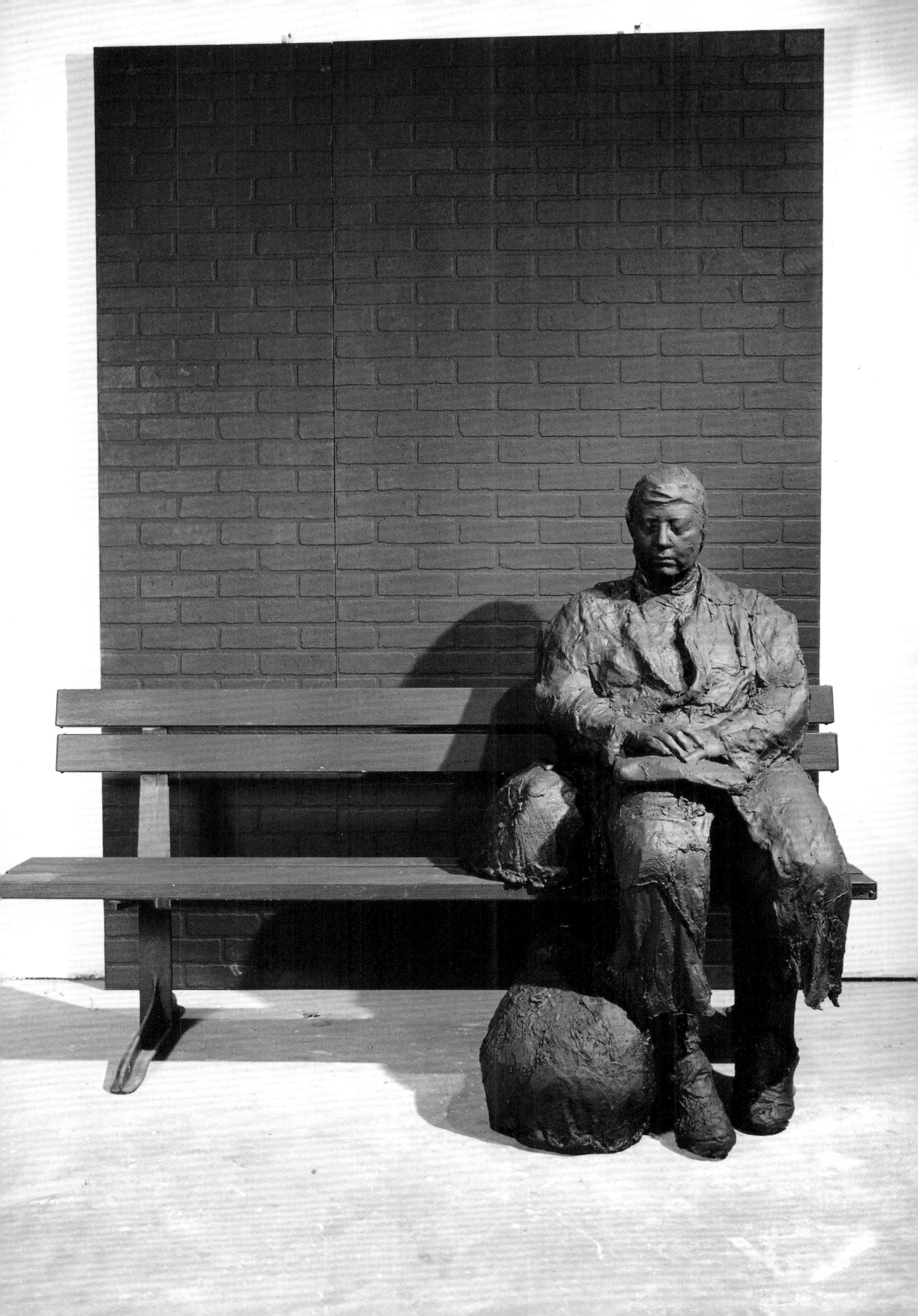

George Segal at Mark Twain
Diner, Union, New Jersey, 1991

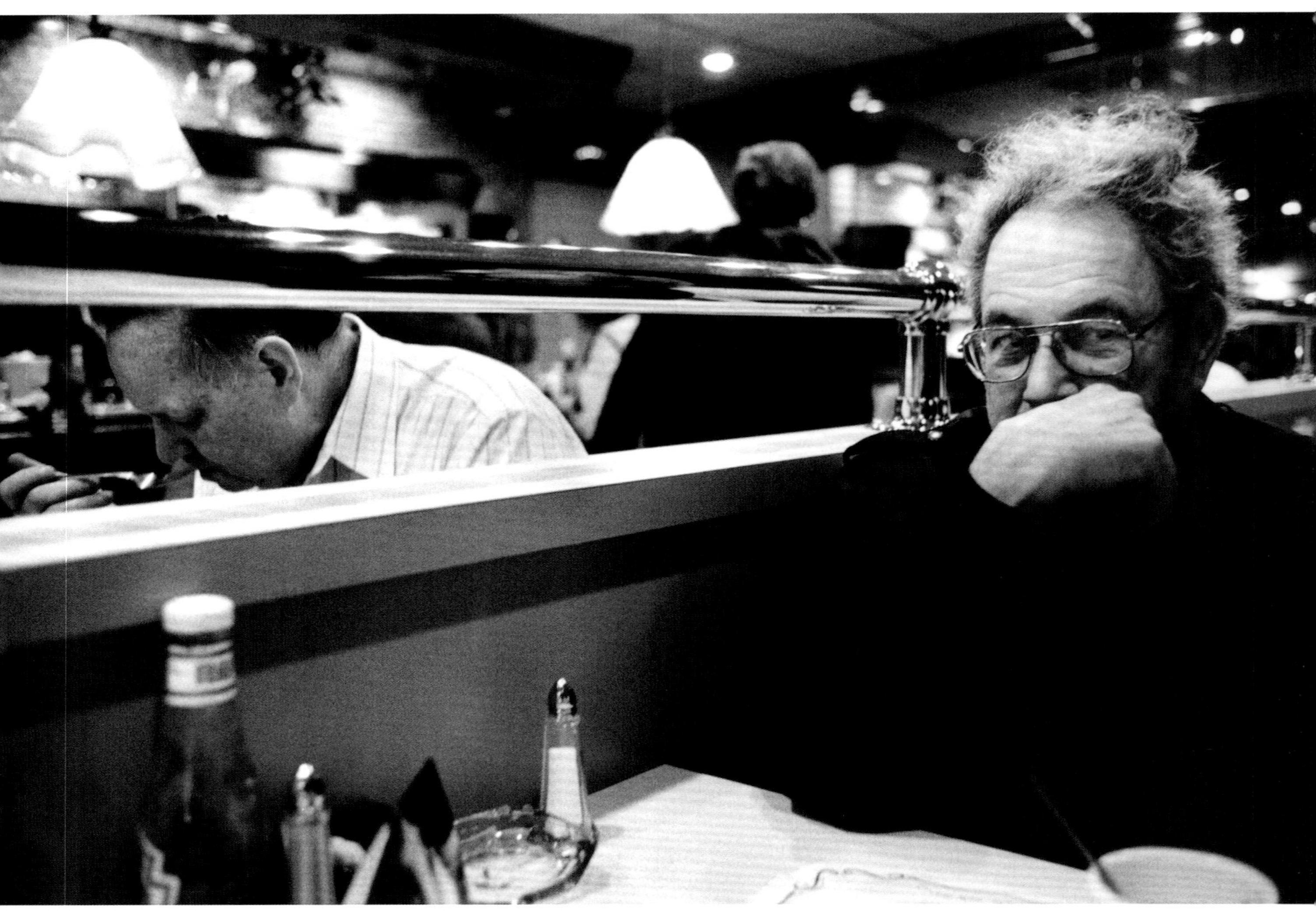

Jane Simon

George Segal's New York

George Segal was born in New York City in 1924.
His parents ran a butcher shop on 174th Street in the
Bronx. By the time Segal was attending Stuyvesant
High School in Lower Manhattan, his family had
moved to New Jersey to run a chicken farm. Although
business was tough for raising poultry, especially
during the war, Segal's left-leaning parents were
fulfilling their utopian dream. Segal, who stayed on
with relatives in New York to finish high school, was
later admitted to the prestigious Cooper Union Art
School. When his older brother, Morris, was drafted in
1940, George moved from New York to New Jersey
to help support his family on the farm.

Segal went on to spend the rest of his
productive life in the bedroom community of South
Brunswick, New Jersey. He married Helen Steinberg,
raised two children, welcomed guests from around the
world, and created seminal works of art on land that
once supported a chicken farm.[1] Segal's home in New
Jersey was adjacent to the sprawling campus of Rutgers
University. Forty minutes from New York, the area
to this day remains rural in aura, suburban in reality—
simultaneously supporting cows and strip malls.
For decades throughout his art career, Segal traveled
by bus into Manhattan. Entering the city through
the Port Authority bus terminal on Fortieth Street and
Eighth Avenue, Segal explored the hidden nooks
of the city with his camera. With friend and sometime
assistant Donald Lokuta, Segal traveled to neighborhoods such as the Bowery and the East Village to
experience the vibe of the city and interact with its
various inhabitants. As a native New Yorker, Segal was
one of them. But as an artist, Segal's role shifted to

*This essay would not have
been possible without the help of
The George and Helen Segal
Foundation and Donald Lokuta*

During the installation of
Depression Bread Line
and **Appalachian Farm Couple**
at the Franklin Delano
Roosevelt Memorial, 1997

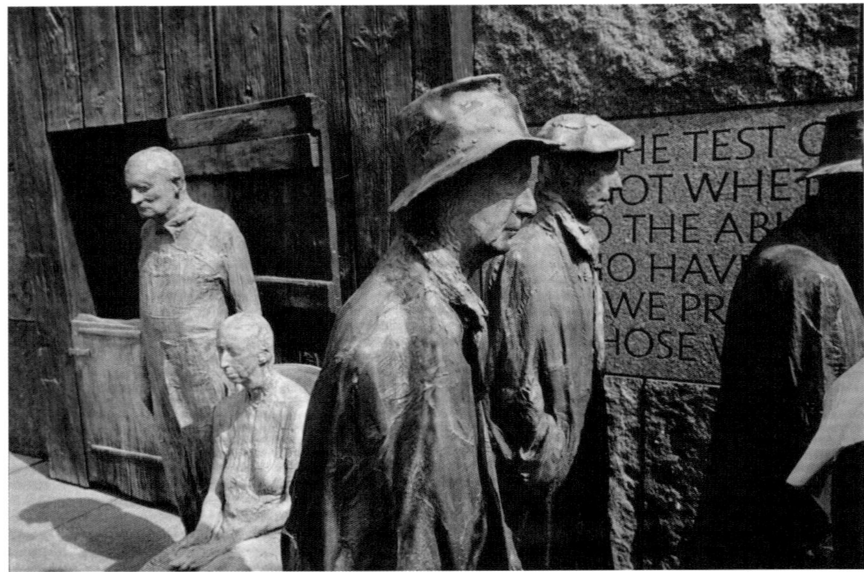

that of observer; he translated observation and insight into sculptural form, rendering vignettes of daily urban life into aggregates of ghostly—but realistic— white figures.

George Segal: Street Scenes focuses on the urban themes embedded in many of the sculptural works Segal completed during his long and illustrious career, exposing his complicated and mediated relationship to New York and American cities as a whole. From the early 1960s, when Segal's work was often associated with the burgeoning pop art movement, through the 1990s, when New York City itself was in transition, Segal made work showing the everyday happenings of the city.[2] From pieces that give form to the arranging of letters on a cinema marquee to ordinary people crossing the street, Segal's works offer a glimpse of real life with real people. Segal's sometimes unsavory figures silently play out believable, realistic scenarios, exposing often-overlooked situations and problems.

Because of Segal's long relationship with the city, *George Segal: Street Scenes* reflects renditions of life as it has evolved through various stages in New York. The urban condition, in both specific and general terms, was alternately exciting and demure to Segal, and he chose to focus on it as both springboard and environment for his exploration of the human spirit. In addition to presenting the unglamorous—even mundane—aspects of the urban environment, Segal also showcased transgressive and alternative behaviors, offering viewers a voyeur's glance at the city and its sometimes illicit underbelly. In his time and to this day, Segal is known as one of America's

most important artists. His works can be found in museums and public spaces around the world, and they are lauded for their accessibility and appeal to a broad spectrum of people. This exhibition reveals the artist's fascination with the darker, seedier side of life.

Segal's art has been the subject of numerous exhibitions in museums and public commissions since the 1960s. In 1978, the Walker Art Center organized a retrospective of the artist at a crucial midcareer point. The brainchild of his close friend Martin Friedman, the show featured Segal's early ruminations on his life in the New York area, such as *The Butcher Shop*, 1965, and his later explorations of biblical themes as they relate to contemporary events, such as *In Memory of May 4, 1970*, an adaptation of the story of the sacrifice of Isaac.[3] The exhibition affirmed Segal's status as one of the preeminent American artists of his generation, whose works addressed the myriad facets of the human condition, from the everyday to the most symbolic and metaphorical. A later show, organized by the Montréal Museum of Fine Arts and curated by pop art scholar Marco Livingstone, combined the early work with later paintings and works on paper. Works such as the seminal *The Subway*, 1968, were on display with draw- ings of his life and friends. The show presented Segal as a working, thinking artist. *George Segal: Street Scenes* is the first major exhibition to explore a single theme inherent in the work of this American sculptor. Using a perspective familiar today—with a keen interest in place, environment, and influence—the exhibition unearths the love affair this American

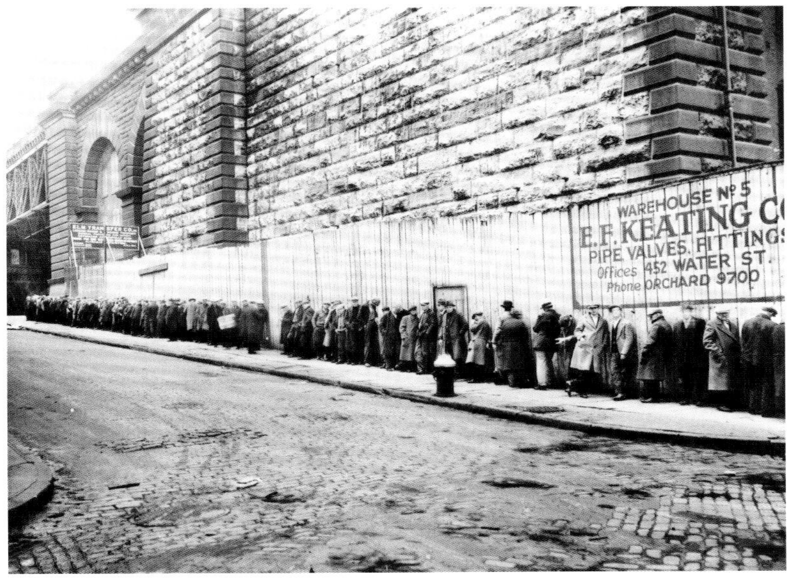

New York, New York.
Bread line beside the Brooklyn
Bridge approach, c. 1930–35
Library of Congress,
Prints & Photographs Division,
FSA-OWI Collection,
[LC-USW33-035391-C DLC]

artist had with the city and his ongoing investigation of the breathing fabric of New York.

Segal's work also adorns our nation's capitol, at the Franklin Delano Roosevelt Memorial. Segal completed three individual pieces for the Memorial, specifically *Appalachian Farm Couple*, 1991, *Fireside Chat,* 1991, and *Depression Bread Line*, 1991 (p. 56). Unlike other monuments around Washington, D.C., these memorials commemorate more than just the achievements of one person or one administration; rather, they capture familiar scenes from the era that Roosevelt represents. Together, these three pieces deviate from the exalted status of other statues of presidents and pay homage to the daily life of Americans in the 1920s, 30s, and 40s. With *Depression Bread Line*, Segal depicts the infamous scene of individuals waiting for food rations against the backdrop of a brick wall with a closed door. The five individuals are all men of different ages, part of a whole, yet each hunched over in downcast isolation. As with many of his sculptures, Segal used his friends to model for the work, the inherent intimacy between artist and model infusing the depiction of an all-too-familiar scene from the Depression. The fact that Segal's installation of the Depression takes place in an urban context connects the work to Segal's formative years in the city. During Segal's childhood, New York, like many American cities, was awash in unemployment, food shortages, and general economic malaise. Segal chose to scrutinize the most heart-wrenching aspect of poverty—that is hunger—and he chose his backdrop to be the hard and soiled surface of bricks. Each of the men wears an overcoat and a hat.

Each stands approximately one foot behind the other staring at the feet and back of the man before him. Each is a different height and a different age. The greenish patina of their faces contrasts sharply with the blackness of their coats and the scene as a whole. Their faces are drawn and worried, and the collars of their coats are crusty and worn as if the artist intended the clothing and the faces to work together as elemental forms. Resignation, fear, and determination simultaneously exude from the work. To individuals who lived through that time, the work is a painful reminder of once-ubiquitous poverty. To younger individuals, the work manifests a poignant and unforgettable history. Without being dogmatic, *Depression Bread Line* serves as a cautionary tale of the personal consequences of social hardship and economic ruin, and conveys that theme through a scene that is both heartbreakingly private and unsentimentally public. Segal's interest in the dynamic of the urban environment and its economic vicissitudes is a topic he would explore in more detail in his later works.

Driving home to New Jersey in the early 1960s, with his wife Helen in the car, Segal spotted a man placing letters on a lighted cinema marquee. When Segal took another quick glance, the man was gone, and what remained was only a ghost image in Segal's mind. Soon after, Segal created his work *Cinema*, 1963 (p. 25). Consisting of a lighted wall with neon letters and the figure of a man stretching to place an *R* on the backdrop, the piece captures the often-invisible mechanics of the city—the unseen or perhaps disregarded labor that changes the signs, lights, and letters that facilitate communication. Like in many

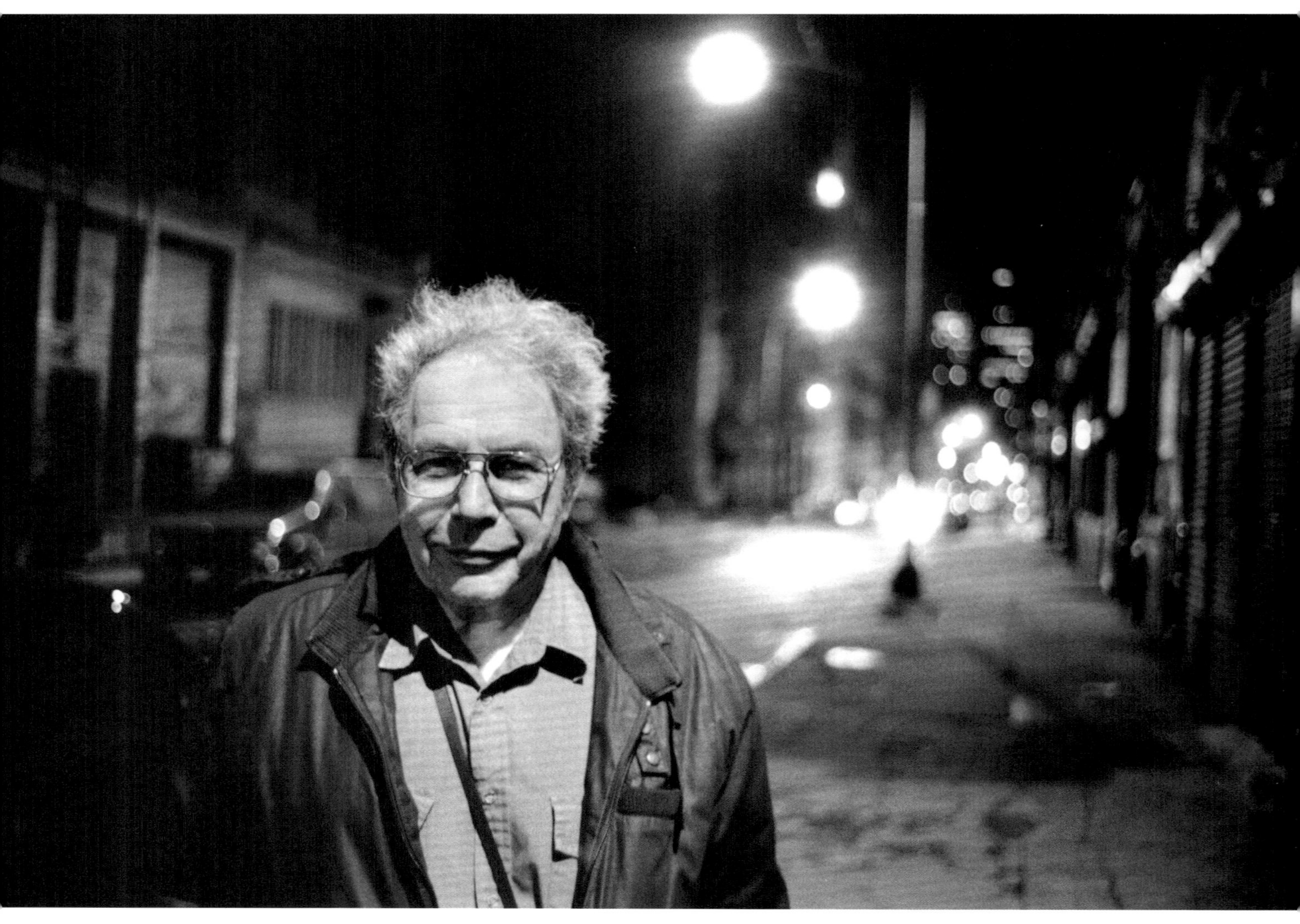

George Segal, SoHo at Night,
New York, 1991

of his other works, this simple gesture exposes
the forgotten venues and toil of the urban machine.
The work also highlights the thoroughfares that feed
into New York and define the modern city. For New
York, the George Washington Bridge and the Lincoln
and Holland tunnels are the most well-known, and
they link the city to the industry of adjacent New Jersey.
These pathways act as the circulatory system of
the city, carrying passengers and goods from the rest
of the world into the New York metropolitan area.
Segal's work functions as a compelling reminder of
the interconnectedness of geography and economy,
travel and labor.

At the same time, the piece surely came out of
the artist's lifetime love of diners and diner food and
his wanderings down anonymous thoroughfares (p. 54).
Segal was a lover of the cheapest and most dingy of
diners. The more down-home the place, the more
he liked to go there. As Donald Lokuta remembers:

Through the years I must have been at lunch a
thousand times with George. When we were away
from the Studio we almost always stopped at a
diner or coffee shop. He was not really interested
in gourmet dining, and he almost never talked

about food. He liked the comfortable and relaxed
environment of a diner, and he fit in with the
people. He was happy with a sandwich, a
hamburger with fries, or something that was on
the lunch special for the day. He always ordered
coffee and almost never ordered desert.[6]

Lokuta recalls a man with down-to-earth tastes who
preferred the workingman's lunch to haute cuisine, the
tawdry diner to lofty design. It makes perfect sense,
then, that in the early stages of his career, when Segal
first began to use found objects and found structures,
he would convert a laminated plastic countertop
into one of the most familiar of public scenarios. Segal
took ready-made parts and objects and molded them
around his lifelike figures. Unlike the other pop
artists of his generation, such as Robert Indiana or
Andy Warhol, Segal's decision to return to the idiom
of everyday life did not grow out of detached irony.
His presentation—to this day—remains sincere.

Segal's 1968 work *The Parking Garage*, similar
to *The Diner* in its sincerity, further uncovers the
critical daily labor of the city. Consisting of a black wall
adorned with a blue square, a large PARK sign created
from red light bulbs, and a white plaster figure, this
work hints at the quiet moments of introspection that
can happen in the bustle of the urban environment.
The figure is sitting quietly on a wooden box, and his
limbs are long with sculpted muscles. His eyes are
cast downward, and fatigue exudes from his posture.
Importantly, the work also lays bare the growth of
the automobile in the United States and the need for
businesses that would cater to the needs of commuters.

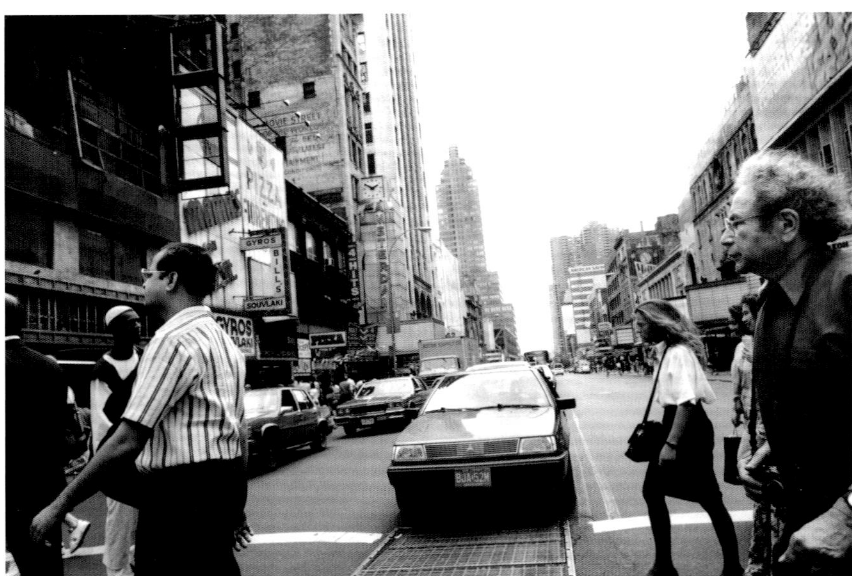

Segal crossing Forty-second
Street, New York, 1990

In this sense, for Segal himself, the work was both personal and indicative of a general phenomenon simultaneously.

During the same time period Segal was composing and erecting *The Diner*, he created two individual works showing a young woman in a doorway. *Girl in Doorway I*, 1965, shows a figure (who was modeled from Helen) dressed casually in cigarette pants and a jacket standing in the doorway of a building (p. 29). The woman seems apprehensive about going out into the night. Her body is situated close to the entryway, and in his analysis, art historian Jan Van Der Marck explains that this work is indicative of Segal's own penchant for tight enclosures.[7] Like many of his early sculptures, *Girl in Doorway I* was also created from found objects. In this case, the artist adapted the materials from a house scheduled for demolition in New Jersey. The doorway seems to have originated from a quaint older neighborhood in Brooklyn, Queens, or New Jersey. The artist has transformed the façade by painting it a luminescent silver. Segal had first tried painting the structure brown, which would have made it a realistic and direct adaptation of common architecture, however, the shiny silver surface suggests a different feeling about the city and the figure in the piece. The sculpture captures the moment just before the young woman enters the night, thereby alluding to other lively happenings in the city. It moves beyond depiction into interpretation.

The dynamism of the city reappears in Segal's *Times Square at Night*, 1970 (p. 61). For this work, Segal created two walking figures and two marquees advertising UNINHIBITED SEX and a Pancake House. Going one step beyond the quotidian scenes of *The Diner* and *Girl in a Doorway I*, this work touches on the sex industry of New York.[8] The two figures are dressed casually and appear to be strolling down the street, replicating the sensation of a sidewalk encounter between strangers. Placing the viewer in the Times Square neighborhood, the work conjures a voyeuristic dynamic in an energetic and, yet, transgressive arena. Because of Segal's ability to capture people as they are and not as we want them to be, *Times Square at Night* touches on the reality of the neighborhood and confronts behavior in American cities that is simultaneously tolerated and taboo. Segal's rendition of this phenomenon is realistic rather than cinematic, down-to-earth rather than glamorous. It is a vehicle and an effect that he would return to continually in the 1970s, 80s, and 90s.

For their weekly jaunts into New York, Segal took the bus, and Lokuta the train. They would meet around Times Square, which is on Fortieth and Seventh Avenue, and then travel to unexpected areas of the city either by subway or on foot (p. 60). Crossing the island of Manhattan, they would eventually make their way downtown, to places like the Bowery. One of the oldest neighborhoods in New York, the Bowery has long been known as a haven for gangs, thugs, and drunkenness. Its own "Bowery bums" became symbols of forgotten individuals in the city.[9] With *The Bowery*, 1970, Segal depicts area vagrants (p. 69). In the sculpture, one figure leans against a green, ridged façade of a building, while another lies on the ground—asleep in a drunken stupor. The standing man, holding

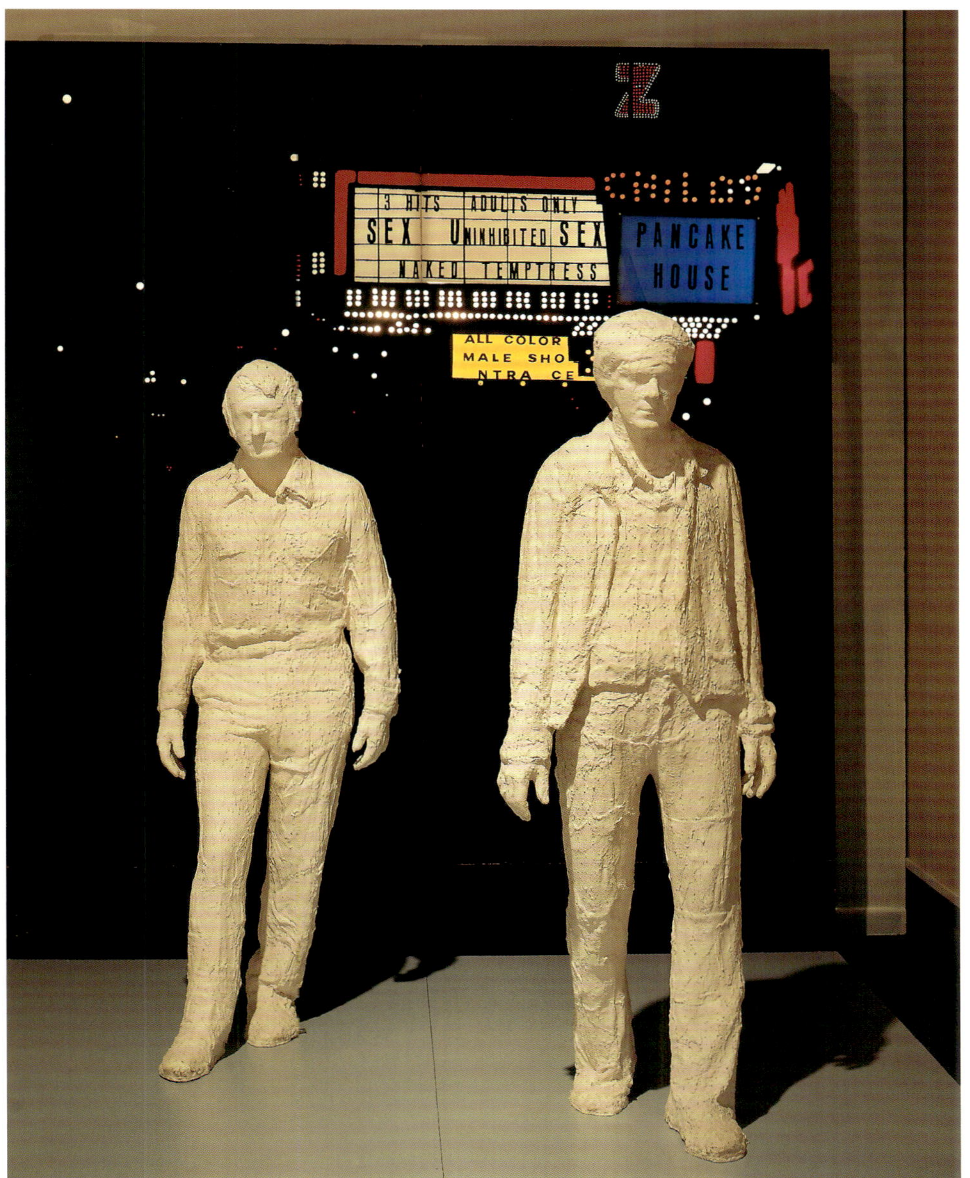

George Segal
Times Square at Night 1970
Plaster, wood, plastic,
electrical parts
108 x 96 x 60 inches
Joslyn Art Museum, Omaha,
Nebraska

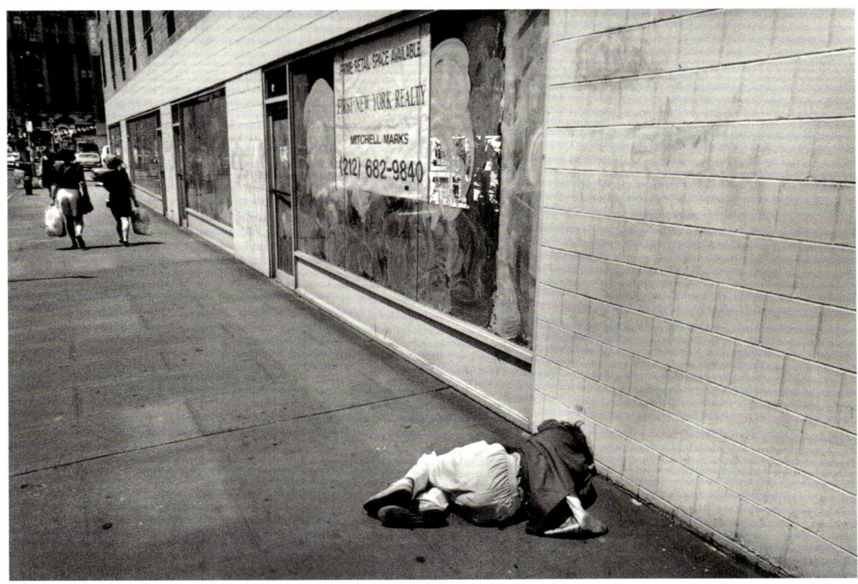

Homeless Man, New York, 1991

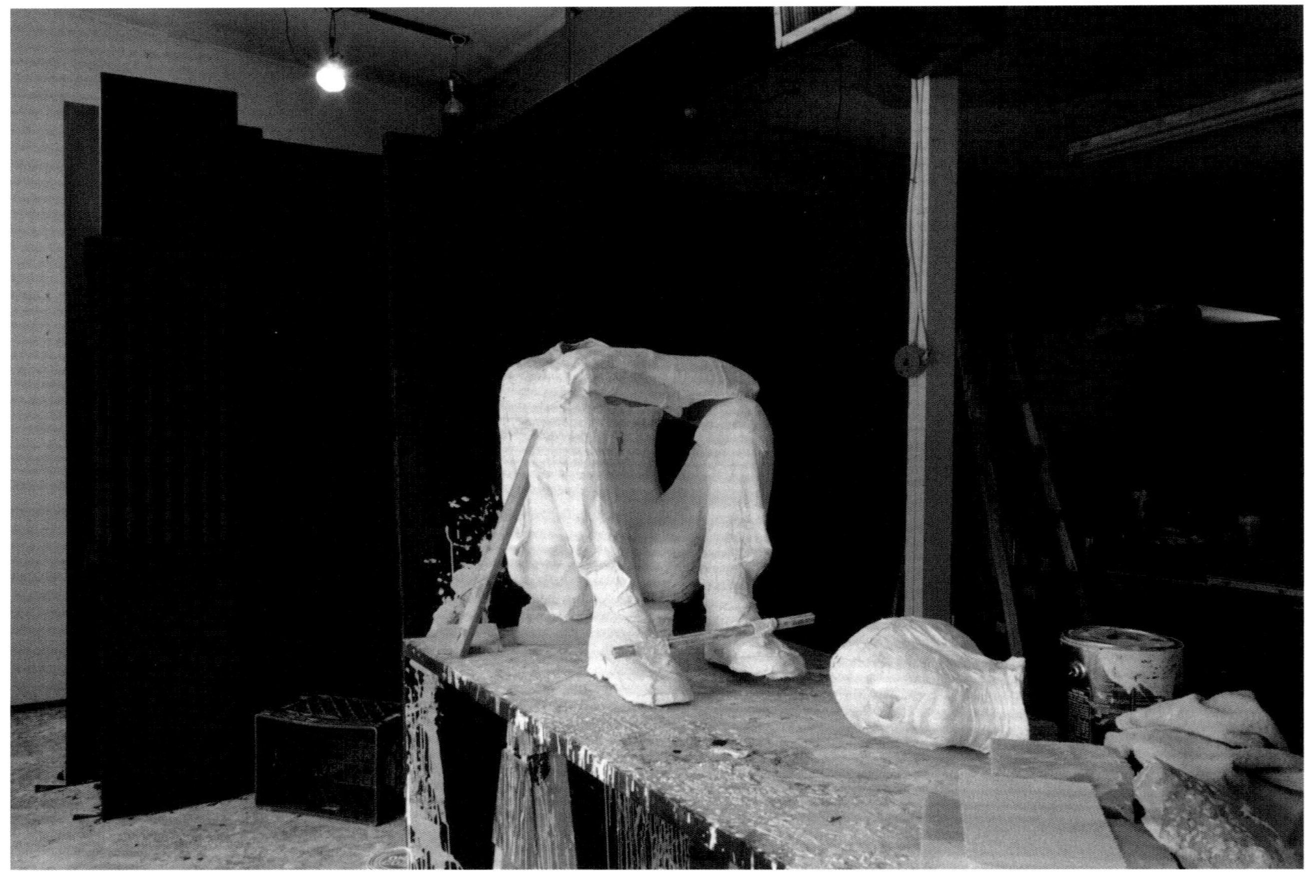

a cigarette in his right hand, regards the other with resignation, but not surprise. He appears relaxed and nonchalant, as though he is passing the time with neither ambition nor scorn. Segal was a contemplative, political man, but he felt no need to proselytize. Instead he infused his compositions of everyday scenes with the intuitive, unblinking grasp of a denizen. With this in mind, *The Bowery* functions as a portrait of urban plight rather than a public service message, and it would set the tone for much of Segal's work in the 1980s and 90s.

Segal's 1989 work *The Homeless*, exemplifies this point. *The Homeless* consists of a man sitting with his back against a brick wall and a figure, draped in voluminous layers of cloth, lying over a subway grate (pp. 40–41). Next to the seated man (actually a plaster

molded from Donald Lokuta) is a bundle of cloth— a symbol of the life of the vagrant and a brief allusion to the hobo sacks of the Depression era. Based on the urban blight of Manhattan's Lower East Side in the 1980s, *The Homeless* renders a tale of misfortune and urban decay. According to Lokuta, Segal often took an interest in the drama of the city. "George was attracted to the ethnic neighborhoods and the activities of everyday life that spill [out] onto the street."[10] Like *Depression Bread Line*, which embodies individuals and confronts the economic devastation of the Great American Depression, Segal's works from the 1980s and 90s capture the hardship of America's urban centers. As white flight and a changing economic climate affected the centers of American cities, a phenomenon known as urban decay spread from East Coast cities

Completed figure for
The Homeless, 1989

below: Segal with figure for
The Homeless, 1989

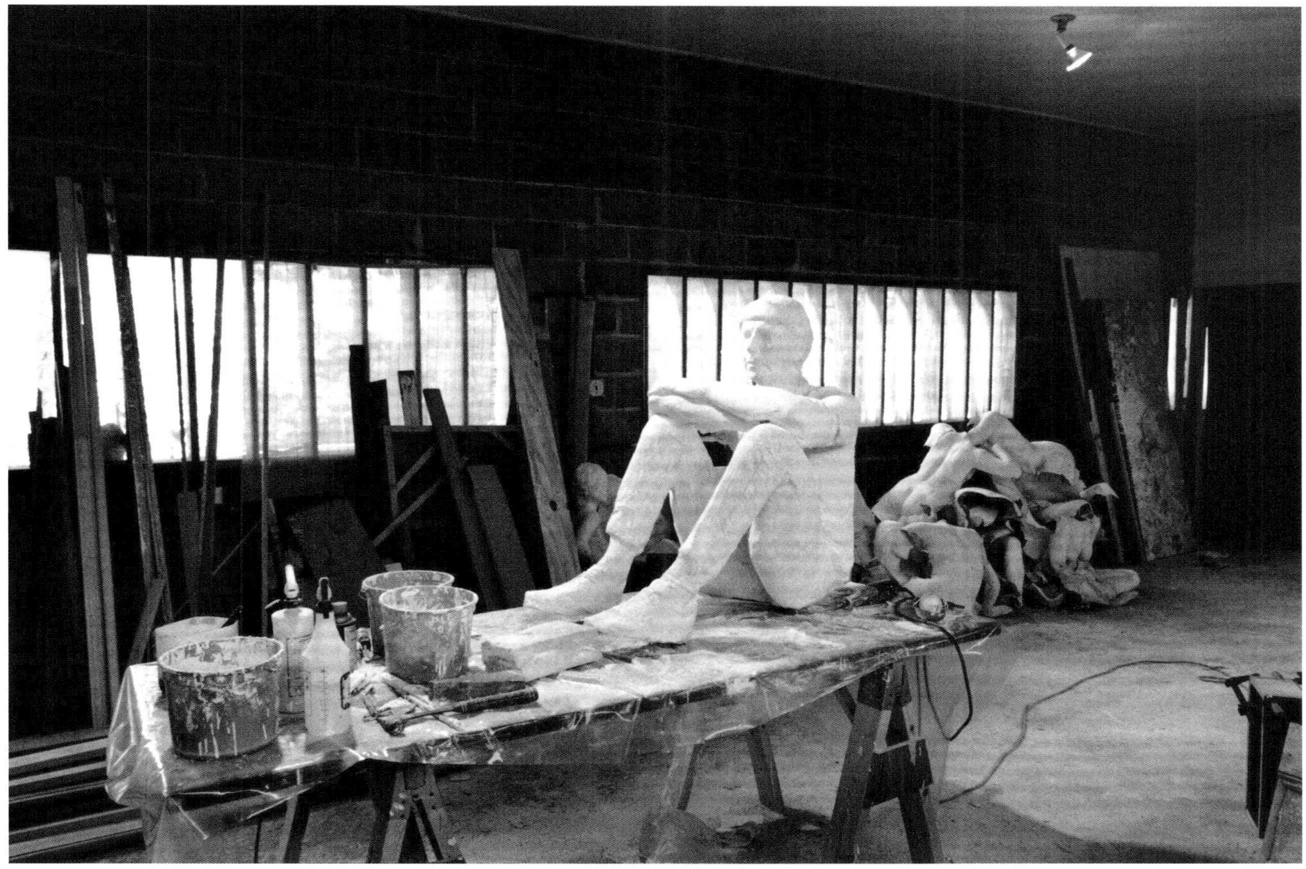

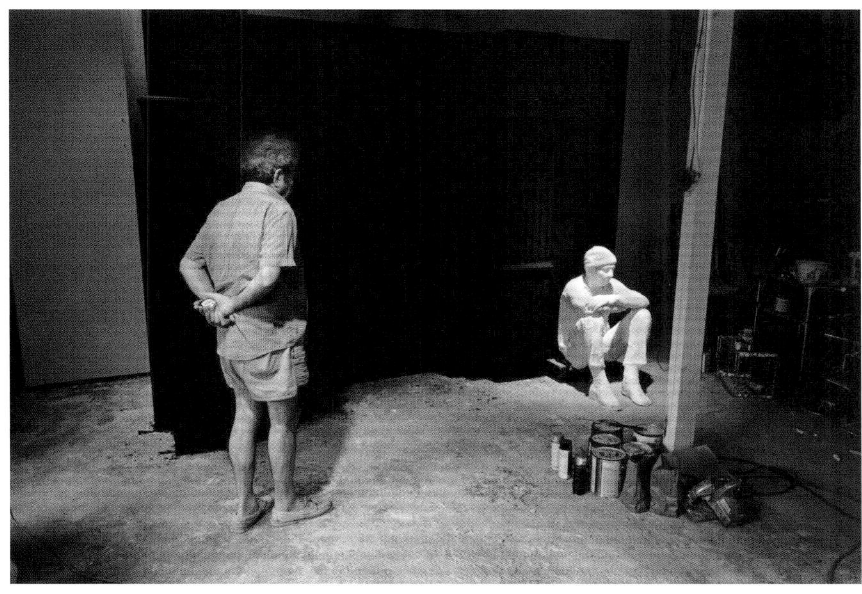

Segal walking on Avenue C,
New York, 1991

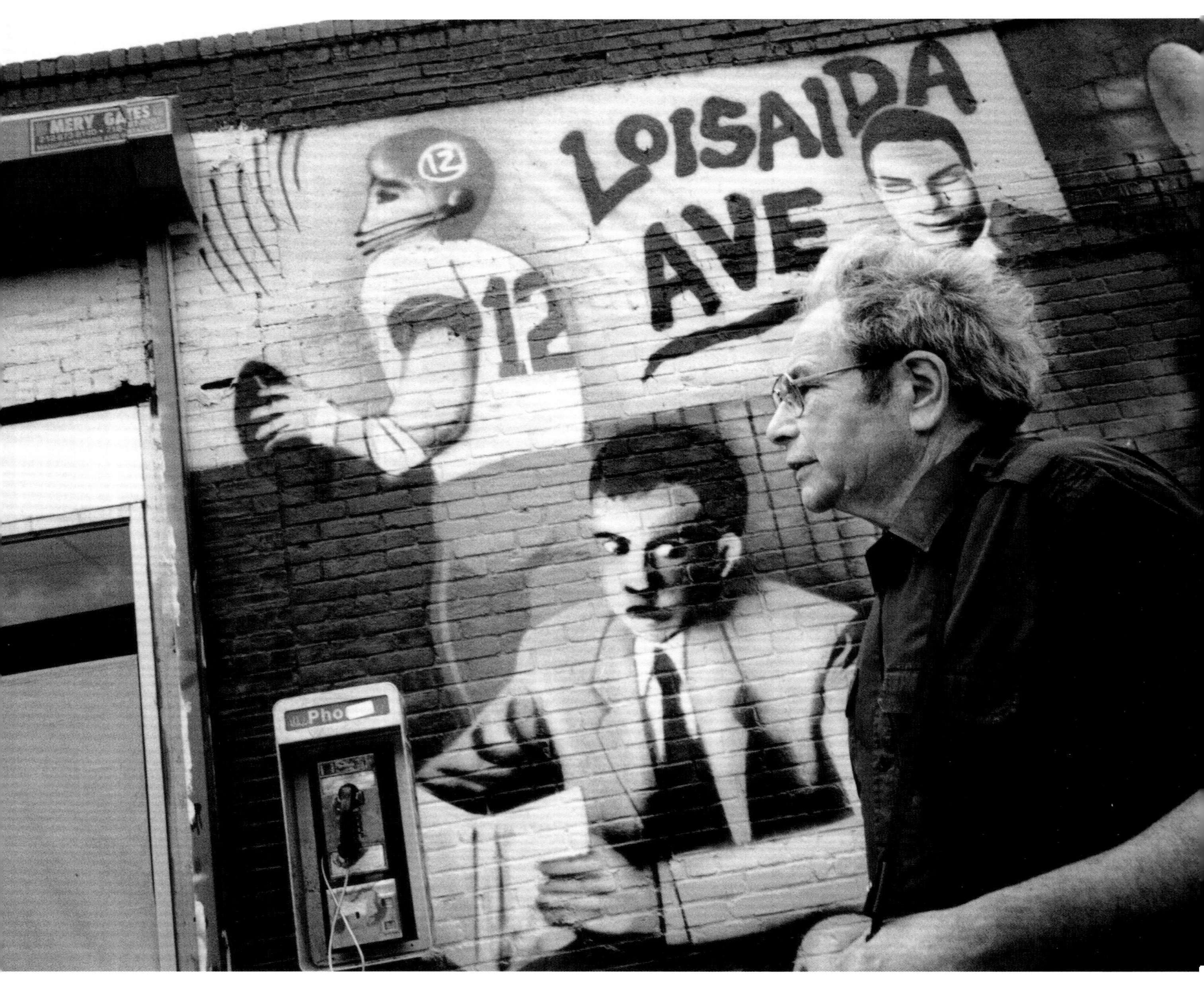

to the Midwest and across the country (pp. 62–63).

Segal was ready to examine and capture the events of New York as it reflected this national trend. By the end of the 1980s, Manhattan's East Village was undergoing tremendous upheaval as it shifted from a state of urban decline to gentrification. Long the home of recent immigrants and the working class, this area of New York has always been known for lively cultural activity and diversity. Stretching from Fourteenth Street south to Houston, and from the Bowery east to the East River, this parcel of New York life includes Alphabet City, Tompkins Square Park, and Stuyvesant Town. Mixing Puerto Rican communities with the last vestiges of immigrant Jewish populations, along with scores of artists, musicians, and bohemians, life in the East Village was exciting and rebellious, creative and illicit at the same time. Segal returned to this cultural breeding ground dozens of times and reflected that personal research in his works from the 1980s and 90s. Lokuta captured many of the trips with his camera, and those photographs serve as a record of Segal's interaction with the changing environment of New York.

At that time, the gentrification of the East Village was slowly clashing with the cadre of squatters, drug dealers, and vagrants of the area[11] (p. 64). When residents of the neighborhood complained of the noise, then-mayor Ed Koch and police commissioner Benjamin Ward sought ways of reclaiming the park for residents. What ensued was a bloody clash between protesters and police, known as the Tompkins Square Riots, and to this day, it is one of the most violent skirmishes between law enforcement and civilians in a contemporary American city. Lokuta readily

remembers how Segal wanted to go into the city, specifically the East Village, the day after the Tompkins Square Riots of 1988:[12]

> One day we each watched on the evening news as the City of New York forced the homeless out of Tompkins Square Park and spurred what was called the Tompkins Square Riots. The city later brought in heavy equipment and demolished and removed the makeshift homes. The video was emotionally moving—it seemed like another country. George immediately called me and said that he wanted to go to Tompkins Square Park the following day. The scene was lonely and desolate. There was really nothing left. I don't think we made any pictures. There was nothing left to photograph and nothing much to say.[13]

It is not clear what Segal thought about this battle, or whether or not he took sides in the debate. What we do know is that he was drawn to this drama and its ensuing transformation, and many of his later works examine the personal terrain of this urban upheaval.

Nestled between homelessness and the abhorrent behavior of this slice of New York, there emerged a particular aesthetic, filled with punk under-tones and real-life examples of urban life (p. 66). Segal's 1994 installation *Dumpster* reflects those two parallel trends. Combining a photographic backdrop with three-dimensional elements, the work simultaneously references reality and perception. The background of the piece shows an image of the city strewn with trash and graffiti, complete with wheat-pasted posters

Razor wire and graffiti,
East Village, New York, 1991

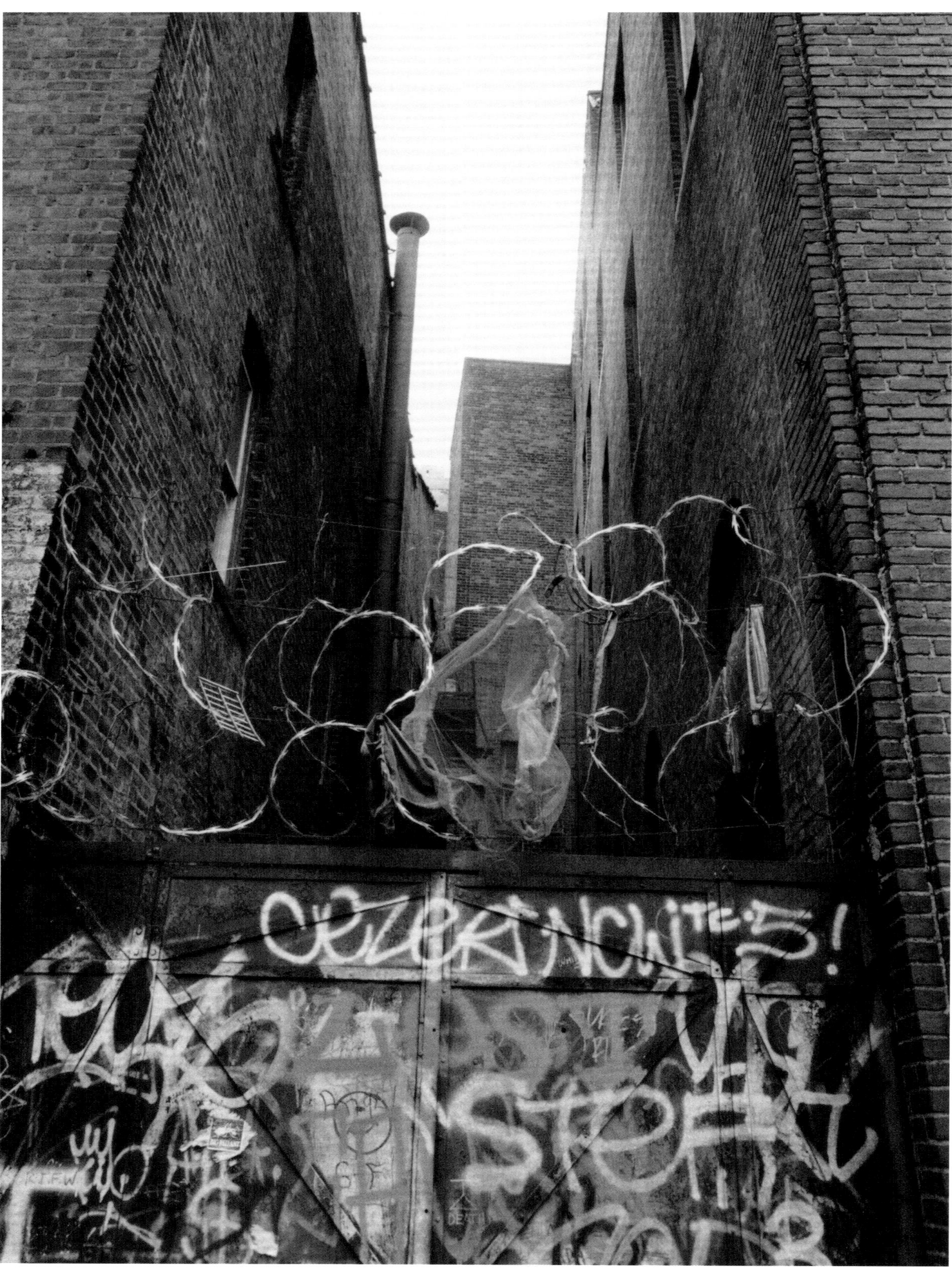

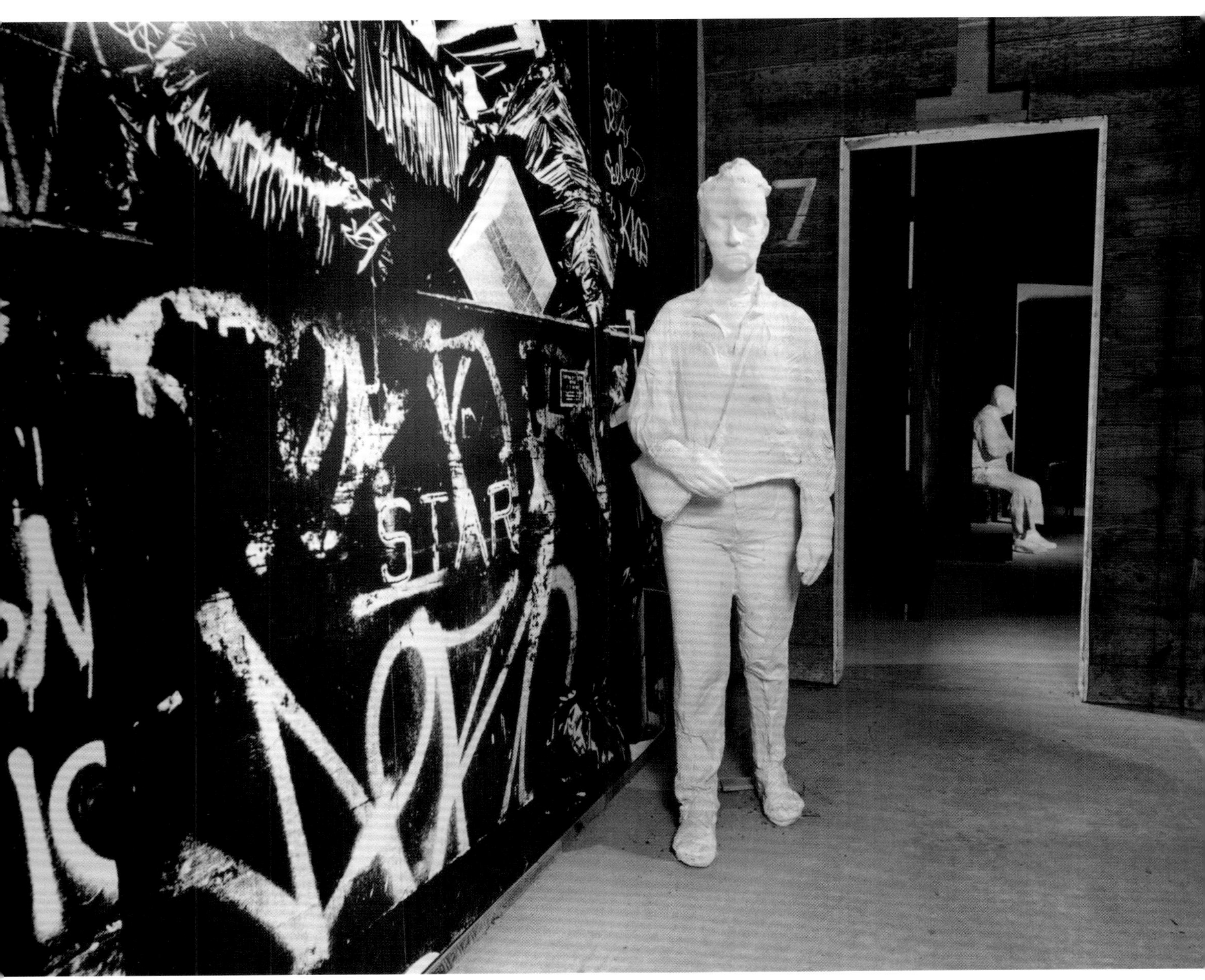

View of room 7 with **Dumpster**,
2000

of emaciated punk-rock figures. In the foreground of the work, walking past these images, is a lone female figure (pp. 46–47). She appears slightly saddened and almost separate from the urban blight in her midst. Clad in plain, casual clothing, she stands in stark contrast to the punk-rock scene around her (p. 67). Along with *Liquor Store*, 1994, Segal seems determined to focus on the forgotten and hidden human stories of New York (p. 49). Sporting a large, documentary-style photographic backdrop, *Liquor Store* shows the figure of a man sitting on a step, glancing at passersby. Despondent and perhaps destitute, this figure is just one of a series of characters Segal created to make his picture of New York a rendition that is about the people and places we tend not to scrutinize. He sought out those urban characters who were not the subjects of novels or stories—but rather those who embody an aspect of the city that rarely draws the focus of the lens. Coming from New York and relishing what it had to offer, it is not hard to imagine that Segal found his muse in the most bohemian of New York neighborhoods. Nor is it hard to imagine that Segal, the guy who left New York as an impressionable adolescent, would return time and time again to the city of his birth.

Toward the end of his life, Segal continued to explore the city and what it meant to live there. In 1997, he completed a series of works about buses and their passengers. One such work, entitled *Bus Passengers*, 1997, shows six figures on a crowded metro bus (pp. 50–51). Three are sitting; three are standing. Three of the figures are petite women of various ages, and three figures are male. All of them seem mildly annoyed by the claustrophobic environment of the bus and its gradual lunge around the city. As a whole, they seem to share an awareness of their collective journey and the bond that exists between them as riders and residents.

Over the course of his prolific and enormously successful career, Segal was often lauded for his ability to capture the core experience of the human condition. More than once, he was chosen to complete large public works because his figurative sculptures— cast from white plaster—appealed to art historians, critics, and the general public. His renditions presented real rather than idealized people. Bringing together the works Segal made with urban themes further explores the motivations and the successes of this great American artist. Knowing that he was born and raised in the largest city in the United States and knowing that he continually explored its neighborhoods and changing drama provides evidence that the city was Segal's muse throughout four decades of art making.

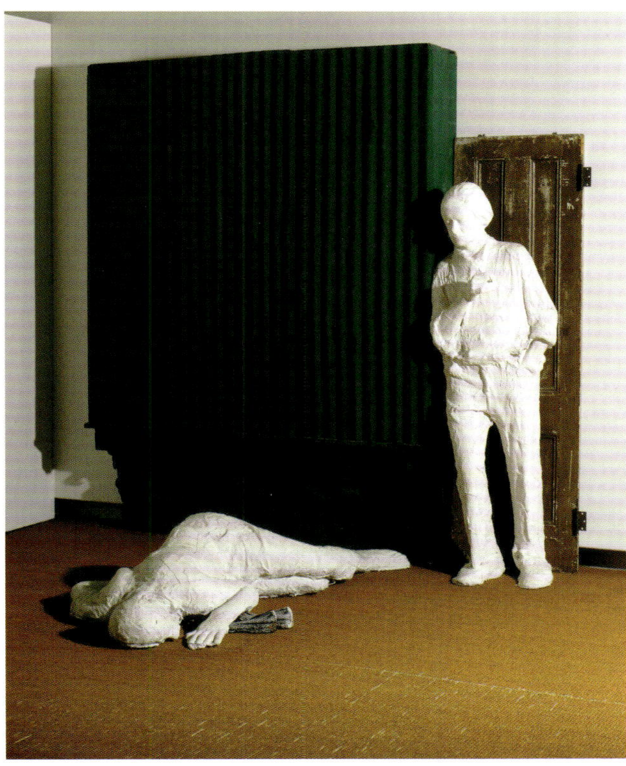

George Segal
The Bowery 1970
Plaster, wood, metal
96 x 96 x 72 inches
Collection Kunsthaus, Zürich

1 Photographs of former president Bill Clinton offer just one example of the illustrious people who visited Segal.

2 Segal was a close friend of Allan Kaprow, the American artist known for creating "Happenings" in the 1950s and 60s. For an extensive explanation of the artistic exchange that came out of Segal's friendship with Kaprow, please see Phyllis Tuchman, *George Segal*, (New York: Abbeville Press, 1983), 12–14.

3 Created for the campus of Kent State University, the work was a sensitive response to the violent protests of the Vietnam War.

4 This quote by Segal appeared in an article Martin Friedman published in *Art International* in 1980. I am indebted to this author and his wonderful scholarship on the artist. See Martin Friedman, "George Segal: Proletarian Mythmaker," *Art International*, 24 (January–February 1980): 19–20. Please see Martin Friedman's essay in this volume for his discussion with the artist about the tension in this work.

5 Later in his career, Segal made a number of works explicitly exploring sexuality, particularly the female body and female sexuality.

6 Donald Lokuta, conversation with the author via e-mail, January 28, 2008. Segal's daughter, Rena, can name the locations and establishments her father frequented around the city, for example one diner called the Red Flame on Fifty-seventh and another in New Jersey called the Spinning Wheel.

7 See Jan Van Der Marck, *George Segal*, (New York: Harry N. Abrams, Inc., 1979), 98.

8 The nature of the business district around Times Square changed radically during the administration of Rudolph Giuliani. For more information, see Jonathan P. Hicks, "Giuliani in Accord with City Council on X-Rated Shops," *New York Times*, March 15, 1995.

9 Many works of art have addressed the Bowery such as Mark Helprin's *Winter Tale*.

10 Donald Lokuta, conversation with the author via e-mail, January 28, 2008.

11 Sarah Lyall, "Residents Clash with Police in Village Park," *New York Times*, August 1, 1988, B3. Robert D. McFadden, "Park Curfew Protest Erupts into a Battle and 38 Are Injured," *New York Times*, August 8, 1988, A1.

12 Dennis Hevesi, "Rally in Tompkins Square Park to Protest Police Action," *New York Times*, August 12, 1988, A1.

13 Donald Lokuta, conversation with the author via e-mail, January 28, 2008.

14 Lyall, "Residents Clash." McFadden, "Park Curfew Protest."

15 Hevesi, "Rally in Tompkins Square Park."

Cinema 1963
Plaster, illuminated
Plexiglas, metal
118 x 96 x 30 inches
Collection Albright-Knox
Art Gallery, Buffalo,
New York
Gift of Seymour H. Knox,
1964
K1964:3

The Diner 1964–66
Plaster, wood, chrome,
laminated plastic,
Masonite, fluorescent lamp,
glass, paper
93 ¾ x 144 ¼ x 96 inches
Collection Walker Art
Center, Minneapolis,
Minnesota
Gift of the T. B. Walker
Foundation, 1966
1966.47

Girl in Doorway I 1965
Plaster, wood, glass,
aluminum paint
113 x 63 ¼ x 18 inches
Collection Whitney
Museum of American Art,
New York
Purchase 65.49

The Parking Garage 1968
Plaster, wood, metal,
electrical parts, light bulbs
120 x 152 x 48 inches
Collection The Newark
Museum, Newark, New
Jersey

Box: Man in a Bar 1969
Plaster, tempera on metal,
wood, cloth
60 x 24 x 12 inches
Collection Museum
of Contemporary Art,
Chicago
Gift of Mr. and Mrs.
E. A. Bergman
1974.12

**Japanese Couple against
Brick Wall** 1981
Plaster, paint, wood
96 x 92 x 27 ½ inches
Courtesy The George and
Helen Segal Foundation,
New Jersey and Carroll
Janis, New York

Restaurant Diner Still Life
1983
Plaster, paint, wood
16 x 33 x 17 ¼ inches
Courtesy The George and
Helen Segal Foundation,
New Jersey and Carroll
Janis, New York

Chance Meeting 1989
Bronze, metal sign
123 x 41 x 55 inches
Courtesy The George and
Helen Segal Foundation,
New Jersey and Carroll
Janis, New York

The Homeless 1989
Plaster, paint, wood,
Masonite, metal
96 x 144 x 52 inches
Courtesy The George and
Helen Segal Foundation,
New Jersey and Carroll
Janis, New York

Depression Bread Line 1991
Bronze
108 x 148 x 36 inches
Collection Madison
Museum of Contemporary
Art, Madison, Wisconsin
Gift of The George and
Helen Segal Foundation
with funds for casting
provided by Bill and Jan
DeAtley, James and Sylvia
Vaccaro, a major grant from
the Madison Community
Foundation, Jim and
Cathie Burgess, the Pleasant
T. Rowland Foundation,
the Overture Foundation,
and Tom and Martha Carter.

Street Crossing 1992
Plaster, paint
72 x 192 x 144 inches
Courtesy The George and
Helen Segal Foundation,
New Jersey and Carroll
Janis, New York

Dumpster 1994
Plaster, silver gelatin prints
96 ½ x 144 ⅓ x 27 inches
Courtesy The George and
Helen Segal Foundation,
New Jersey and Carroll Janis,
New York

Liquor Store 1994
Plaster, wood, acrylic paint,
silver gelatin prints
104 x 156 x 62 inches
Courtesy The George and
Helen Segal Foundation,
New Jersey and Carroll
Janis, New York

Bus Passengers 1997
Plaster, metal, plastic
80 ½ x 68 x 52 inches
Courtesy The George and
Helen Segal Foundation,
New Jersey and Carroll
Janis, New York

Woman on the Bench 1997
Plaster, paint, metal
96 x 72 ½ x 37 inches
Courtesy The George and
Helen Segal Foundation,
New Jersey and Carroll
Janis, New York

Hot Dogs 1997
Plaster
2 x 6 x 4 inches (each)
Courtesy The George and
Helen Segal Foundation,
New Jersey and Carroll
Janis, New York